H 23

'THE NIGHT THE C

C000183654

'A Taste Of Cyprus'

By

Androulla Christou-Layton

and

Michael Layton

Copyright © 2017 by Androulla Christou-Layton and Michael

Layton.

First Published by Bostin Books June 2017

Paperback Edition by Bostin Books September 2017

Front Cover photo: 'Andry' 1983.

Cover design by Stephen Burrows

Table of Contents

Foreword

Looking East & West

Androulla Christou-Layton was born in Cyprus in 1965 some fifty-one years ago – it is her home and where her heart truly lies.

Greek is her first language and she is rightly proud of her Greek Cypriot heritage.

She was born on an island where the lives of families are inextricably linked, and whatever the distance between them the bonds remain strong.

One of the first things that Cypriots will do when meeting for the first time is to establish where each other's parents originate from and it is very unusual for some family connection not to be found. It's one of the things that makes them unique as a nation.

The Cypriot character can appear to be quite fiery, at times, and to the unknowing spectator a room full of Cypriots involved in animated conversation can sometimes look more like an evolving public-order situation.

People express their feelings in a very open, and sometimes emotional manner and what would be a totally normal situation for them might well appear to some to be quite a lively environment to say the least!

What they don't do however, is harbour negative feelings for very long, and whilst a day might start with an argument in the morning it will invariably finish in the evening with a meal and normality restored.

More commonly known by her shortened name of 'Andry', she has tried to capture some of these characteristics within this book.

**

Cyprus is an island covering an area of over nine thousand square kilometres, and is the third largest in the Mediterranean after Sicily and Sardinia.

It is routinely referred to in Greek as *'Kypros'*.

The island stands at the far-eastern limits of the Mediterranean and has a rich blend of European and Eastern influences as it stands at the crossroads of three continents.

Archaeological finds indicate that the island was populated by the sixth millennium BC, at least, with Neolithic art being found from the period 5800-3000 BC.

The Neolithic settlement of Choirokoitia, on a hillside above the Limassol to Larnaca road, is marked by a bee-hived shaped stone and is said to be the site of the first mud-dwellings that Cypriots lived in.

To the west of a hill called Vounaros, in the village of Trachoni, near Limassol, ancient artifacts have been recovered which indicate that this was also the site of a Neolithic settlement.

Its history has been shaped by the Roman, Greek, and Turkish Empires, and more recently by the outcome of an invasion, and its membership of the European Union.

Roman and Greek archaeological sites can be found in abundance in Cyprus, many of them in the area of Paphos, where there are mosaics from the 3rd and 5th century on the floors of noblemen's villas showing scenes from Greek mythology.

Mosaics of Dionysos, the god of wine, Theseus slaying the Minotaur, and Orpheus playing his lyre, which were created in the first few centuries AD, have been discovered, together with the Tombs of the Kings.

Cyprus is a country which looks truly to the east, and west, at the same time in terms of how its culture and traditions have been shaped.

The Greek influence on the island stretches back three thousand years when the Achaeans brought their religion, and their language, as well as politics. The so-called 'Hellenism' of the island remains a strong factor even in today's society, and many still see Greece as the natural 'motherland'.

What they also brought with them in the 13th century was their gods, the most important of whom was the Goddess Aphrodite – the goddess of female beauty with a lust for love.

This is her legend:

'Aphrodite was born in Paphos in Cyprus. She is said to have been the daughter of Zeus, and Dione, and the wife of Hephestus. A slightly different version of mythology has her emerging fully-clothed from the sea at Paphos, where flowers grew in her path, and she was attended by Eros, appearing as a baby with wings, together with Peitho and The Graces. According to the legend she was not faithful to her husband and had the power to make all the other Gods fall in love with her, with the exception of Athena, Artemis and Hestia. She also loved mortal men such as Anchises to whom she bore a son. She punished both Gods and mortals alike who offended her .

Just outside Paphos in the sea, not far from the beach, is a large rock known as 'Aphrodite's Rock', which is where they say that Aphrodite rose from the foam of the waves when Cronus divided the god Uranus into two parts. The Greek word 'aphros' means foam and 'dite' translates to 'I come out' hence the name.

Aphrodite is represented as a celestial being, as well as universal.

She is also considered as patroness of the seafarers and is sometimes accompanied by a swan.'

People believe that if they can swim around the whole of the rock, at Petra tou Romiou, they will have a long life – it is not as easy as it looks and most fail!

Statues exist, in museums, of Aphrodite in different poses riding a dolphin, framed between two seashells, and holding a child. In yet another one Pan is shown trying to embrace Aphrodite who threatens to hit him with a sandal as a little Eros flies between them.

The area of Geroskipou is known as *'Ieros Kipos tis Aphrodites'* the *'Holy gardens of Aphrodite birthplace.'*

Also to be found in Paphos is St. Paul's Pillar where the Saint was reputedly captured, tied-up and lashed.

***

During the Lusignan period, between 1192 and 1489, the Catholic Church replaced the Greek Orthodox Church, but it survived despite severe oppression.

It was during this period that large numbers of Maronites arrived from Lebanon and settled. They remain a minority in Cyprus to this day. Between 1348 and 1349 there was a serious outbreak of plague on the island which led to the deaths of a third of the population.

***

The Venetians then took over in 1489, after the last Lusignan Queen of Cyprus, Queen Catherine, gave up her rights to the Republic of Venice.

Shakespeare's tragedy *'Othello'* is connected to the Venetian occupation of Cyprus, and is said to have taken place in the tower of the old town of Famagusta. Built in the 15th century an effigy of the *'Winged Lion Of Venice'* sits over the front entrance.

The tower where Othello, a Moorish warrior, who was in the service of the ruler of Venice, murders his *'Desdemona'* is known as *'Othello's Tower'*.

It was here that Othello smothered his wife after accusing her falsely of adultery, before committing suicide.

***

The Venetians remained until the Turkish Ottomans invaded in 1570, using 100,000 soldiers, and three hundred ships, and the island fell after a long siege, the following year in 1571.

One of the island's last defenders, Marc Antonio Bragadino, the Captain of Famagusta, had his nose and ears cut off by his captors, on the 5th September 1571, before being flayed and stuffed with straw!

At that time the population of Cyprus was estimated to be some 200,000.

The Greek Orthodox religion was restored, although their Turkish rulers used the Church to help in the collection of taxes.

A Muslim minority was integrated into the population, although they paid 10% of their produce in taxes, whilst Christians paid between 20% and 50% in taxes.

In 1660, a very significant act took place when the current Sultan recognized the Archbishop of Cyprus, and three Bishops, as political leaders and representatives of the Cyprus people. The position of the Archbishop as the *'Ethnarch'*, or national leader, placed the Greek Orthodox Church in a very powerful position, which was certainly used during the discussions with the British in the 1950s.

To this day the church in Cyprus is extremely influential and occupies a very visible presence in every town, village, and corner of society.

The duty of a priest is to help the vulnerable, and the poor in the community, as well as conducting the church services on a Sunday, and celebrating *'name-days'* christenings, weddings, and funerals.

In the Greek Orthodox Church men who are already married are allowed to become priests but single men who become priests are not allowed to marry later in life.

They are very visible with their full-length black robes and black hats.

***

On the 4 June 1878, a treaty was signed between Great Britain and the Ottoman Empire on the basis that Britain would supply weapons to Turkey in the event of another war with Russia.

The Treaty was known as the *'Defensive Alliance between Great Britain and Turkey'* and was signed by the British Prime Minister Benjamin Disraeli and the Sultan.

In return Turkey handed over Cyprus to Great Britain for an annual sum of £92,799, eleven shillings and three pence to be paid to the Sultan.

The amount was later paid by Cypriots in taxes!

Under the auspices of the 1878 Cyprus Convention, Britain assumed administration of the island, and the first British troops arrived in Cyprus.

The following year in September 1879 the Cyprus Military Police was formed to replace the old system of *'zaptiehs'* who were predominantly Turkish Muslims.

Recruitment was opened up to Christians, or non-Muslims as they were referred to then, and by the following year the Force consisted of just over six hundred officers with two-thirds distributed across six districts of the island on foot patrols.

In 1879 the idea of *'Enosis'* raised its head in Cyprus, for the first time, when the concept of a formal union with Greece was promoted by some of the Greek Cypriot population.

In geographical terms Cyprus lies more than 950km from the Greek mainland and the nearest Greek island is Rhodes, which is some 400km away. Clearly distance was not an issue in the eyes of those who supported the concept.

When the British took over there were no roads in Cyprus and some of the harbours were silted up. An early proposal was put forward to build a railway line but it was 1905 before one was actually constructed.

That first line connected the capital Nicosia with the port town of Famagusta, in the east, and was some thirty-six miles in length.

In 1914 Turkey entered the First World War on the side of Germany and as a consequence Britain declared the earlier treaty null and void. The island was annexed by the British on the 5 November 1914, at which point it became part of the British Empire.

When the Treaty of Lausanne was signed in Switzerland on 24 July 1923 Turkey renounced all rights to Cyprus, which was then declared a British Crown Colony on the 1 May 1925.

***

In 1932 the railway line was extended to Morphou, to the west of Nicosia.

In 1937, after several reorganisations, the Cyprus Military Police became the British Colonial Cyprus Police, and adopted a police rank structure. This Force was to play a key role in future events on the island.

During the Second World War some 35,000 Cypriots volunteered to join the British Army to fight against the Germans, which many saw as a fight for freedom and democracy.

Many of them died at the Battle of El Alamein in Egypt in 1942.

At the end of the war in 1945 Cypriots saw no change to the existing status quo and calls for unification with Greece grew once again.

***

On the 15 January 1950 a referendum was organized in Cyprus by the *'Ethnarchy'* Church Council on the question of *'Enosis'* – union with Greece. This resulted in 215,108 people signing in favour at Greek churches throughout Cyprus - 95.7% of those entitled to vote.

Once again nothing changed and indeed in 1954, during a debate in the Houses of Parliament, a member of the British Government made it clear that because of its strategic importance the island would never be considered for self-determination.

With the advent of the motorcar the railway system, such as it was, went into decline and the whole system closed down in 1951. To this day the vast majority of Cypriots rely on private transport rather than the limited public transport facilities in existence.

Today's modern Cypriots have a habit of wanting to park as close to their intended destination as possible, and perfection is getting their vehicle literally outside the front door of the premises they are visiting. They will strive for nothing less and public transport fails to satisfy this culture.

***

What has been described as a national liberation struggle started on the 1 April 1955 as members of the *'National Organisation of Cypriot Fighters'*, known by its Greek acronym of *'E.O.K.A'* set off a number of explosive devices across the island.

Archbishop Makarios assumed the political leadership of the group and Colonel George Grivas was responsible for military operations. Grivas used the pseudonym *'Dighenis'* after the 11th century Byzantine legendary hero *'Vasilios Dighenis Akritas'*.

During the course of the violence police stations were routinely attacked, sometimes bombed, and at times taken over by EOKA fighters. Police officers were murdered and members of the community perceived to be working with the British were assassinated.

Somewhat significantly EOKA murdered two hundred and thirty Greek Cypriots as opposed to one hundred and five British soldiers, who were amongst those deployed across the island.

EOKA fighters and supporters also lost their lives as the British Administration struggled to crack down on the armed group.

In the summer of 1956 racial tension flared up between Greek and Turkish Cypriots, with most of the latter being opposed to the concept of Enosis. The auxiliary police force which supported the British forces, was made up predominantly of Turkish Cypriots.

The troubles were to last until 1959.

***

On 9 March 1959 George Grivas issued a proclamation calling for all members of EOKA to lay down their arms and to accept the political agreements that had been reached.

He returned to Greece shortly afterwards and received a number of honours, including being promoted to the rank of General.

A number of prisoners were released by the British in the same month, including a man by the name of Nikos Sampson, who had been in prison in England. On his return to the island he was likewise welcomed as a returning hero – a man who was to feature again significantly in the history of Cyprus in years to come.

***

On the 16 August 1960, Cyprus, in accordance with the Zurich – London treaty, was granted independence from Great Britain, who retained two fifty square mile areas of strategic importance, which are still classed as British Sovereign Bases at Akrotiri and Dhekalia.

The Republic of Cyprus was thus born at two minutes past midnight on that date in an official ceremony, which took place in the conference room of the Transitional Committee that later became the House of Representatives building.

Shortly before midday, at Government House, the Union Jack flag was run down and the Cyprus flag raised, thus ending eighty-two years of British rule.

The new flag portrayed neutral colours, neither the Greek blue, or the Turkish red, and featured the map of Cyprus in yellow with two green olive branches underneath, and on a white background.

The emblem of the new Republic was a dove with an olive twig in its beak, which was designed to symbolize peace and co-existence.

The evidence and influence of the previous British rule is however still very visible within the country today. Vehicles are driven on the same side of the road, English is routinely spoken by many as a second language, and the legal system has retained many similarities, not to mention the thousands of English people who have made Cyprus their permanent home and the many thousands of English tourists who visit every year.

***

On 20 July 1974, Turkish armed forces invaded the northern area of Cyprus, on the pretext of coming to the rescue of the minority Turkish Cypriot population, and more than one third of the island still remains occupied today, with estimates of more than thirty thousand Turkish troops stationed in the north, and more than two hundred thousand people displaced.

Nicosia, the capital of Cyprus, is divided by the so-called *'Green Line'*, running across the Old City from east to west, policed by a United Nations Peace Keeping Force. It is a place where time stands still and the contents of some shops, houses and restaurants remain exactly as they were left as the area was hurriedly evacuated in 1974.

Since 2004 it has been possible to cross from one side to the other via crossing-points in Nicosia which have been established for people on foot at Ledra Street, or by car at the Ledra Palace Hotel.

Also in 2004 the island became a member of the European Union.

***

Less than a million Cypriots actually live in Cyprus, and rumour has it that more Cypriots actually live in other parts of the world, than live in their home country. In the UK alone there are estimates of up to 300,000 living in the country, and there is a sizeable population in Australia.

The majority of the population in Cyprus is comprised of Greek Cypriots (Approximately 80%) whilst there is a sizeable minority of Turkish Cypriots (Approximately 18%). The remainder includes Maronites and British Ex-Patriots (2%) many of whom are of state pensionable age and can take advantageous of dual-taxation arrangements, as well as the better climate.

Each year that population is inflated by more than two million visitors to the island eager to experience the sun, the sea, and the scenery. For those who look beyond the tourist areas there is much to experience.

Many of the English visitors make for Paphos which is pronounced in Greek as *'Pafos'*, whereas English people often refer to it as *'Pathos'* which is in fact the Greek word for *'passion'*!

The main centres of population in the so-called *'free areas'* of Cyprus are Paphos, Limassol, Larnaca, and Nicosia, whilst many Cypriots still live in local villages that retain a very personal sense of identity, and culture.

Coffee shops and tavernas provide traditional meeting places where men in particular, in the former, can catch up with all the gossip and argue about football and politics.

Cypriots love talking, and love eating even more, and the saying goes that they, *'eat each meal as if it is the last day of their lives and build houses as if they are going to live forever'*.

There are many unique features to local Cypriot food, for example Cyprus desserts, which are best accompanied with a Cyprus coffee, and a glass of cold water. The so-called *'spoon-sweets'* are made with fruit such as walnuts *'karidaki'*, or bitter oranges, bergamot, grapefruit, watermelon, apricot, or cherries and many others, often in syrup.

Conversely Cypriots build houses *'as if they are going to live forever'* and with one eye on the neighbour's house will always be keen to make sure that they finish up with an impressive building!

Greek Cypriots overwhelmingly follow the traditions and teachings of the Greek Orthodox Church. The apostles Varnavas, and Paul, preached the new Christian faith in Cyprus in 45 AD and founded the Church of Cyprus.

Religion still shapes their lives from birth to death and the Church maintains a very powerful voice, and influential voice, amongst the people.

They say that three things are pre-ordained by Cypriots at birth, the first of which is religion. The second is the nature of the political party they will follow, which in turn influences the football team that they will support. These things are passed on from father to son, and mother to daughter.

Quite often the names of children are also pre-ordained, passed down from grandparents to new-born children, and it is also common practice for names to be shortened during everyday conversations.

This book begins with the creation of a new Greek Cypriot family and then charts the first eighteen years of the life of Androulla Christou-Layton, in this beautiful country.

It provides a very personal insight into how, during these years, many Cypriots lived relatively simply with the constant feel and smell of a sea-breeze, and the calming waters of the Mediterranean never far from sight. The pressures of life are now somewhat different but the principles remain the same.

Even today the opportunity to see and smell the sea remains a very important element of the psychology of Cypriots, most of whom do not take kindly to a totally urban style of living.

This book recounts the story of how the '*Christou*' family grew and lived through tragedy, poverty, and political instability, and yet survived.

***

Much of this book is told in Andry's own words, and as importantly in her own style of English. It also incorporates recollections from other members of her family, particularly her

mother, as well as other Cypriot friends, and previously untold recollections from two members of the British Armed Forces who were on the island in 1974.

Above all else this book is a tale of hope and happiness, notwithstanding the journey through births, christenings, marriages and even deaths as the story unfolds.

A simple way of life riddled with cultural complexities.

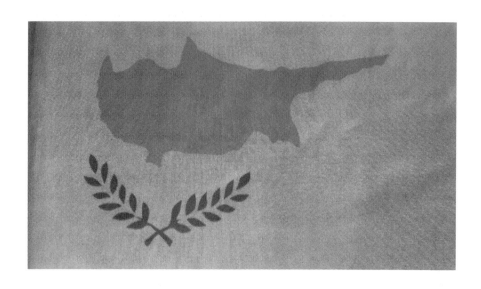

Figure 1 The Cyprus Flag

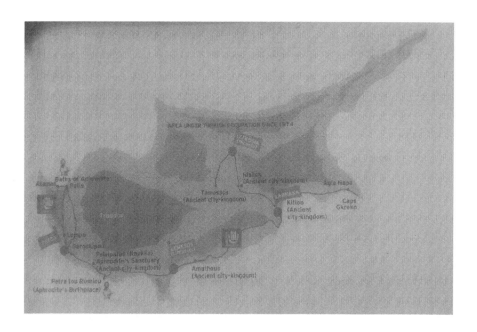

Figure 2 Map of Cyprus

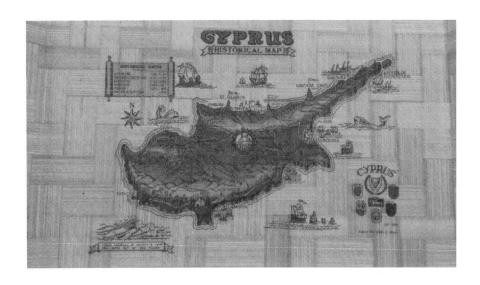

Figure 3 Map of Cyprus

Introduction

The Creation Of A New Family

Andry's father, Costas Christou, came from the small village of Kythrea, once the ancient city of Chytroi, which is 10 km northeast of Nicosia.

It is an archaeological area of some significance, by way of example an outstanding bronze statue was discovered in the area of Roman Emperor Sepimius Severus (193-211), which is now exhibited in a museum in Nicosia.

The statue depicts a stocky completely naked man with a beard and short curly hair.

After its Greek Cypriot inhabitants were displaced and made refugees in August 1974 the town was re-populated by displaced Turkish Cypriots, mainly from the area of Alaminos.

Alaminos village itself used to be a mixed community and is about 28 km from Larnaca. In 1960 the population of 564 inhabitants were split almost equally between Greek and Turkish Cypriots, but ultimately the 251 Turkish Cypriots relocated.

The area was known for growing tomatoes, cucumbers and artichokes.

Prior to the Turkish invasion Kythrea was home to the football club AEK Kythreas. Millions of gallons of water a day flowed freely from the nearby Kephalovryso Mountains and some believe that the water originates in the Anatolia Mountains in Turkey and reaches Cyprus by subterranean routes.

The story goes that at some point after the Invasion this water stopped flowing but the reality is that because lots of water extraction was allowed in the area many of the natural water tanks dried up.

(Andry):

"My father's father, Christos, was twelve years younger than his wife Irinou when they got married. He was in his twenties and she was in her thirties, which was unusual in those days.

My grandfather wanted to marry a woman with white skin who had a strong build body because according to his beliefs she would be able to manage better working within the fields where a woman's main job was to scythe the wheat. He also thought that a larger woman would be better for bearing children.

Usually the way it worked was that the eldest daughter in the family married first but Irinou had an older sister who was much less beautiful than her so the men wanted the second daughter first.

As long as the first daughter was not married none of them were to be married. The parents of families were very involved in arranging marriages then and had a heavy influence on the decision-making.

My father's father was also known as *'Mavris'* by all of his friends because he had very dark skin. It comes from the Greek word for black, which is *'mavro'*.

My father was born on the 23 April 1937 and he was the fourth child of four sons."

***

Andry's mother, Loukia Christodoulou, was born on the 28 October 1936, in the village of Choulou, also referred to as Houlou, which is in the District of Paphos, and sits at an altitude of 350m above sea level. The name of the village comes from the founder, and first settler of the area, who was from Syria. Its main characteristics are narrow streets, and stone built houses, with two stone-built bridges in the middle of the village along Argaka Way.

In the period of the Frankish rule in Cyprus Houlou was a small feudal town, and in the Middle Ages was home to *'Arodafnousa'*, a beautiful woman, who became involved in a love/hate drama of the time which is now part of Cypriot folklore.

Her story is told as follows:

'According to legends she was one of three very beautiful daughters in the town. She was so beautiful that no-one could believe it. Every morning when she woke she used to sing songs by her window, looking at the forest and waiting for her nanny to comb her hair. One day Peter the French king of Cyprus passed by her window and was immediately struck by her looks. They fell in love and she became his mistress. From that day on every day at the same

time he passed by her window and sang her a love song. One day somebody from the castle came to her house and told her that the Queen Eleonora wanted her to come and stay at the castle. She accepted because this meant she would be close to her love, but at some point he went on a long journey, and her happiness did not last long as the Queen was very cruel to her. Whilst he was away the Queen sent Arodafnousa to a monastery, where she was placed in a small room, like a prison cell, and left. The King later went to some monastery's to pray and found her in one of them weak, pale, and close to death. She told him that she had never stopped loving him and then closed her eyes and died. After her death all of the bells of the monastery rang out and crowds gathered to say goodbye. She died for her love for him'.

There is a plant, found in the Paphos area, known as the 'Arodafni' bush which has very beautiful flowers but is actually poisonous. If the plant gets cut up with the hay in fields it can poison the animals. They say it is like the love of Arodafnousa which was poisoned by others.

By 1946 figures show that some seven hundred and three Greek Cypriots lived in Houlou, together with one hundred and seventeen Turkish Cypriots.

By 2001 that figure had reduced to around one hundred and ninety in total, with much of the village abandoned, but today many of the original buildings have been renovated to attract tourism.

The village has five churches namely Timios Stavros, Ayios (St.) Kononas Chapel , the Venetian church Agias Theodoras built in the 8-9th century, the Byzantine church dedicated to Saint Georgios built in the 12th Century, and Panagia Pantanassa Church built in the 13th century.

There was a Turkish Cypriot minority living in the area until 1964 with clear evidence that both Greek and Turkish Cypriots co-existed in harmony, with a mosque situated in the village. When inter-communal riots began however the Turkish Cypriots abandoned the village to go to areas where there were bigger Turkish Cypriot populations, in the belief that there was safety in numbers.

Just outside the village is the Ammati forest, which is an area of great natural beauty. *'Chorkadiko'* grapes, both red and white, with seeds in the middle, were grown in the area for making wine.

***

There is evidence of wine being produced in Cyprus for more than 5,000 years, with wine jugs thought to be from that period having been recovered on the island, in villages in the Limassol region.

The most famous wine is *'Commandaria'* also known as *'Nama'*. It is a sweet wine and was said to have reminded Marc Anthony of Cleopatra's kisses, so much so that he gave the whole of the island to his legendary lover. This wine is grown on the southern slopes of the Troodos Mountains, and is used as the Holy Communion wine in Greek Orthodox churches.

'Nama' was renamed after Richard the Lionheart sold Cyprus to the Knights Templar. The Grand Commandarie itself was the estate of the Knights of Kollosi.

There are more than one hundred varieties of wine in Cyprus with the most well known grapes being *'Mavro'* and *'Xynisteri'*.

***

(Andry):

"Within the village after each grape harvest season they would have made *'soutzioukos'* which are long threads of almonds or walnuts dipped repeatedly in thickened grape juice and dried in the air. The tradition lives on to this day. The long brown bumpy strings look a bit like rubber but they are very tasty and usually cut up into little round pieces to be accompanied by *'Zivania'* to keep warm in the winter. There is also a creamy version of *'soutzioukos'* with lots of almonds and nuts on top called *'ppalouzes'* and a plain version called *'kkiofteri'* that could last through the winter and be eaten like a snack."

***

(Andry):

"The mother of my mother was named Antigoni. She was a Greek Cypriot but born in Egypt. She came from a wealthy family and she came on a holiday to the village of Houlou with her parents.

The name Antigoni originates from Ancient Greece and according to legend she was the daughter of Oedipus and Jocasta. It sometimes means *'unbending'* and is also referred to as *'instead of mother'*.

Antigoni was only fourteen years old and my mother says that she was very beautiful. She was already engaged to be married to someone else in Egypt. It was the custom then to give their word between families once the child was born. It was a practical arrangement designed to ensure financial stability within families and nothing at all to do with feelings or love. It was purely a business arrangement and those most affected by such arrangements had no say in the matter.

Whilst she was in the village one day Antigoni came into a situation whereby my grandfather had sex with her. According to my mother it was not with her consent.

His name was Christodoulos, and was also known as Takis. He came from a big family in the village and had altogether five brothers, and two sisters. My grandfather was quite a lively person and was always being punished by his father for his misbehaviour.

His family was a priest's family, his father Papa Michaelis was a priest, as was his father before him, and a brother Papa Avramis.

When Papa Michaelis found out about what had happened he took out his priest's hat and cursed his son for destroying the girl's virginity. He demanded that Christodoulos marry the girl. My grandmother's family only agreed with this because they were going to go back to Egypt and intended taking my grandfather with them.

After the wedding however they discovered that my grandfather had a criminal record and was not allowed to leave the country, so my grandmother had to stay in the village, whilst her parents went back to Egypt.

In truth it was a tragedy.

My grandmother was not used to village life and found it very difficult. They were washing clothing in the river, and living a hard life. By the age of fifteen years she delivered her first child, a boy, Aristotelis, and by the age of eighteen years she delivered my mother.

My grandmother could not manage the life and eventually she left my grandfather and went somewhere else to live. My grandfather was a gambler who was always playing cards and was never at home. He lost all his property on gambling whereas all of his brothers and sisters were quite well off.

When she left, Antigoni took my mother with her but my grandfather found them. He took my mother away from her and didn't let her see her children.

He was very strict with this situation and even sometime later when Antigoni's parents came to visit again once he refused to let them take her to visit Antigoni.

My mother initially grew up with her aunt Katerina – one of his sisters, who she used to call 'mum' as she couldn't remember too much about her biological mother.

Takis divorced and re-married when my mother was five years old as Katerina was going to get married herself.

He only did this to have someone to look after his children. His new wife Despina, also known as Pinou, was older than him and at the time it was said that she had no children of her own, although there was another rumour that she had previously had two children who became sick and died. Apparently they had chickenpox and she left them home alone to go to work.

Rumours and stories in Cyprus are a feature of life. Everyone has an opinion on everything and will usually happily share it with anyone who will listen!

She was very slim and short, and had long black hair which stayed that way until she died, without ever having to colour it. She always had her hair in two 'fish-plaits', which she pinned around her head like a wreath.

After they got married she was always hiding her money in the house in different places as she didn't want my grandfather to find it because of his gambling.

Either way this woman did not have a lot of experience of growing up children and mistreated my mother and uncle. But she was afraid of my grandfather so she did not physically abuse them as she knew that there would be consequences.

Pinou used to wear a lot of gold jewellery around her neck, and arms, and although she always introduced my mother to people as being her daughter, comments were often made about the fact that she wore all the gold and my mother wore nothing.

My first-cousin Stella remembers that at the end of the services at Easter Pinou would always bring boiled-eggs in baskets to the church so that after midnight they could try to break each other eggs. Whoever broke the shell at one end won the game.

On one occasion when my mother was growing up in the village she wanted to go across the river to get something. She took a donkey but when she got to the river it was flooded so she tried to cross at its narrowest point which unfortunately was also the deepest. In the water the saddle came off and she finished up hanging onto the donkeys reins until it pulled her back out and saved her. She nearly died and would have done so had it not been for the donkey.

My mum was worrying for the donkey because he was wet and cold but not for herself.

At some point the family moved to Geroskipou and my mother had a lot of Turkish Cypriot friends as a child who she was very close to. She wouldn't stop playing and go to eat unless they ate as well.

My mother's closest Turkish Cypriot friend was named Safie and her mother was Katrie. When there were troubles between Greek and Turkish Cypriots the Turkish Cypriots left the village, in the middle of the night, and went to Mandria where there were lots of other Turkish Cypriots and they felt safer.

The village of Mandria is situated in the south-west coastal region of Cyprus and is thought to have been founded more than five hundred years ago by Turkish Cypriots who called it *'Yeslonna'* which translates to *'green plain'* with reference to the variety of crops that grow there.

Up until the late 1950s Greek and Turkish Cypriots live side-by-side but in the early 1960s up to forty Greek Cypriot families left after feeling threatened.

Conversely, after the invasion took place all the Turkish Cypriots went north to the *'occupied areas'* and the village was repopulated by Greek Cypriots.

During the troubles Safie's father and two brothers were killed by Greek Cypriots.

At one point the brother of my mother's father filled his lorry with sand to make it heavy and protected like a tank. It was a terrible time for everybody.

My mother only went to school until third grade and was unable to write properly. My grandfather took her out of school, at about eight years of age, and put her somewhere to be taught sewing. He said that he only wanted his son Aristotelis, also known as Telis, to go to school, as girls didn't need to know these things.

This was not unusual in Cyprus at that time as male domination was everywhere and women were encouraged to stay at home. Even in church, men stood in the front part of the church and women remained at the back.

Eventually Aristotelis left home at the age of thirteen years to go and find his real mother in Famagusta and didn't come back until he was sixteen years old.

One day my mother was in the village and this person came up to her riding a bike and asked her to get on the back. She refused thinking he was a stranger because he had a moustache and a beard but when she realised it was her brother they started crying together.

Eventually, when my mother was nineteen-years of age, and her father couldn't stop her anymore, she met with her natural mother Antigoni, and they kept in touch.

At the same age my mother went to live in Nicosia and whilst she was living there she was working as a housekeeper at the Ledra Palace Hotel.

The hotel is in central Nicosia and was built between 1947 and 1949 by Cyprus Hotels Ltd at a cost of nearly a quarter of a million pounds, on what was then called Kind Edward VII Street.

It originally had ninety-four bedrooms and was rated as the largest deluxe hotel in the capital before the invasion when the hotel fell within the boundaries of the United Nations Buffer Zone, which was created after a truce was declared. It now serves as accommodation for UN peacekeepers.

At the hotel she was working with my father's niece who took her to Kythrea one day where she met my father. He always says that the minute he saw her he fell in love with her and wanted my mother.

Eventually he took her to Kythrea and told his parents that he wanted to marry my mother and after that they went on a motorbike to Paphos to tell her parents and to make the arrangements.

It used to be customary for the parents of the bride to give a dowry to their future son-in- law and the village priest would witness the formal agreement. If it was later breached the son- in-law had the right to take his father-in-law to court. The parents of my mother and father were poor and as far as I know they had no money to make such an agreement.

***

My parents were married on the 19 August 1956 at Agias Paraskevi Church in the village centre in Geroskipou.

My father was nineteen years of age, and my mother was also nineteen years of age but six months older."

***

(Andry)

"The actual wedding of my parents was on the Sunday but the celebrations took place over three days during the Saturday, Sunday and Monday. My mother has told me the story of what took place.

The Saturday was for preparations and people came to help whilst violins were played, and a Laouto, which looks like a large Bouzouki.

The word Bouzouki comes from the Turkish word *'Bozuk'*. The instrument was brought to Greece in the 1900s, by Greek immigrants from Asia Minor. The front of the instrument is usually flat and inlaid with mother-of-pearl. It is played with a plectrum and has a sharp metallic sound a bit like a mandolin, but pitched lower. They either have three or four strings.

After the preparations everyone sat down to eat.

Sunday was for the ceremony.

Monday was for cleaning and for eating again.

In those days the custom was to deliver a candle to each household to invite them to a wedding. People visited before the ceremony to deliver *'kanishi'* which were gifts such as rice, pasta, and live chickens, all the food to be eaten during that period. The whole of the village were invited.

The practice of giving out invitations, in large numbers, to weddings survives to this day and it is not unusual for hundreds of people to attend, and sometimes thousands – all of whom have to be fed.

On the Saturday there was a fight at the house my parents were renting. Some relatives from Houlou came with some sheep and goats and took them to my grandfather's house.

After they had been slaughtered, by hanging them upside down and slitting their throats, my step-grandmother Despina took some of the meat and kept it to cook for her relatives who were coming later.

Finally she didn't do anything and the meat started to smell next day so she took it to my mother's house where the other meat was and threw the smelly meat into the rest and ruined it all.

My mother's older brother Aristotelis, was furious and wanted to beat my step- grandmother. My grandfather grabbed a knife to attack his son, and my father grabbed my grandfather from behind to stop him. Everyone got involved and at one point my father jumped out of a window and ran away thinking that he was going to get stabbed himself.

This is an example of how emotions can quickly rise to the surface but in this case the prospects of a fight were real!

At this point everyone was wondering whether he would come back and whether there would be a groom at the wedding!

Finally my mother's brother went and found him and brought my father back to the house where all the aunts were busy cooking *'kleftiko'*, potatoes, and *'ressi'*, a special dish that is traditionally made for weddings.

'Kleftiko' is a traditional lamb dish, wrapped in parchment paper, which is slow-cooked in an oven with potatoes. The name comes from the *'Klephtes'* who were war-like brigands who lived in the countryside when Greece was part of the Ottoman Empire. They used to steal lambs, and goats, and cook the meat in covered pits in

the ground in order to seal in the flavours and smells, as well as trapping smoke to avoid giving their hiding-places away.

'Ressi' is made from wheat cooked with chicken or lamb. It looks a bit like a pudding. Traditionally lamb or other meat is slowly cooked over burning embers in large cauldrons until the meat and wheat berries are soft and become a thick pilaf.

It used to be cooked two days before a wedding whilst musicians played and people danced. If lamb was being cooked they would wait until it fell off the bones before being added to create the pilaf.

At the wedding only my grandfather on my father's side attended because my grandmother Irinou didn't want my mother in the family, and made her views very clear.

My mother wore a full-length white dress with a white veil, which she borrowed from a friend who had also recently married. She carried a bouquet of flowers which included roses and dahlias. She had long black curly hair which was mostly hidden by the veil. She looked very beautiful.

My father wore a dark blue suit, with polished black shoes, and had a small flower in his left lapel. He was just a bit taller than my mother and had a pencil thin moustache and black hair.

He was wearing a tie and looked very handsome.

On their wedding photo, which was taken later in a shop, they both looked very serious but I am sure that they were both very happy.

The priest who did the wedding ceremony was my grandfather's father Michaelis. My mother loved him deeply and years later she named her son Michalis in his memory.

Initially my father had no job but my grandfather helped them and then he worked for my mother's brother Telos driving a lorry and delivering sand and gravel for construction work.

My mother got pregnant a couple of months after the wedding and my sister Maria (Maro) was born on 28 May 1957.

She had a difficult pregnancy and delivery as she was suffering from 'lefkoma' a condition that develops and affects your blood pressure.

Maro was christened in a small church outside a monastery, and on the day of the ceremony it was raining heavily.

In those days the custom was for the mother not to go to the church and to wait at home for the child to be brought back to her after the ceremony. The mother receiving her baby after being baptised had to go down on her knees three times and kiss the hand of the godmother, or godfather, in recognition of their role as to being a *'second parent'* if anything happened to the real parents, as well as being responsible for teaching the child the Christian Orthodox religion.

That's all changed now though and mothers now attend christenings.

My mother remembers Maro as being a bit greedy when she was breast-feeding her. Maro started vomiting a lot and my mother took her to the doctors thinking that she was sick. The doctor laughed at her and said that it was just that Maro was taking too much milk and was simply vomiting the extra that was too much for her stomach to take.

As a child Maro always kept her toys untouched and new as she grew up.

***

Just over a year after the wedding my mother and father moved to Nicosia after he had an accident in the lorry whilst carrying ice. My mother's brother Aristotelis was upset about the accident, as his lorry had a lot of damage to it, and so my father got upset as well and they left Paphos."

***

In the 1950s Greece began to raise the issue of *'self-determination'* for Cyprus in the United

Nations, however at this stage the British government were reluctant to de-colonise the island, which was, and still is, of significant strategic importance to them in the Middle East.

In 1955, a *'pro-enosis'* organisation was formed in Cyprus, which favoured a formal union with Greece, under the banner of *'Ethniki Organosis Kyprion Agoniston'* (National Organisation of Cypriot Fighters), more commonly known as *'EOKA'*.

All members of EOKA had to take the following oath:

'I swear in the name of the Holy Trinity that:

I shall work with all my power for the liberation of Cyprus from the British yoke, sacrificing for this even my life.

I shall perform without question all the instructions of the Organisation which may be given to me and I shall not bring any objection, however difficult or dangerous these may be.

I shall not abandon the struggle unless I receive instructions from The Leader of the Organisation, and after our aim has been accomplished.

I shall never reveal to anyone any secrets of our Organisation, neither the names of my chiefs nor those of any other members, even if I am captured and tortured.

I shall not reveal any of the instructions which may be given me, even to my fellow combatants,

If I disobey this oath I shall be worthy of every punishment as a traitor, and may eternal contempt cover me'.

***

There are many recorded incidents relating to the struggles, and one of the most high-profile occurred on the 3 March 1957 when the hide-out of the deputy leader of EOKA, Gregoris Afxentiou, was discovered in the mountains of Macheras, by British Forces who surrounded it.

Afxentiou sent his fellow-fighters out, but refused to surrender himself.

British helicopters were then deployed to pour petrol over the hide-out which was then set alight, burning Afxentiou alive inside.

Whilst many Greek Cypriots were promoting *'union'* and many Turkish Cypriots, some of whom also belonged to a right-wing organisation called *'Turk Mudafaa Teskilati'*, known as *'The Turkish Defence Organisation'* supported *'partition',* one thing that they shared in common was an extreme dislike of communists, whether they were actually real or just perceived.

***

55

By way of an example of the complexities of the struggle, on 23 May 1958 a suspected Greek Cypriot *'traitor'*, who in fact later turned out to be entirely innocent, was subjected to a particularly barbaric attack.

The *'arrest'* of Savvas Menikos was ordered by an EOKA District Leader and he was tied to a eucalyptus tree in the village square, outside the church in Lefkoniko. He was then stoned by a crowd of people, and accused of being a traitor for allegedly telling children off for shouting *'Long live EOKA'*.

He died of his injuries and history has determined that the allegations had no foundation.

***

In 1958 a number of Greek Cypriots with left-wing views were murdered who favoured independence rather than union.

In the summer of 1958 communal violence again erupted, and between June and August alone fifty-six Greek Cypriots and fifty-one Turkish Cypriots lost their lives.

***

In one final example of how different forces were at work during this period on the 12 June 1958 about twenty Greek Cypriots returned from Nicosia to their village in Kontemenos but complained that Turkish Cypriots in the mixed village of Skylloura had impeded their journey.

Twenty-five Greek Cypriots then made their way to Skylloura in two groups but were intercepted by British troops and taken to Yerolakos Police Station.

They were then driven back to the Turkish village of Gonyeli and dropped off in some fields where they were told to walk the four miles back home to Kontemenos.

Some two hundred Turkish Cypriots then surrounded them, armed with various weapons, and attacked them, resulting in eight of the Greek Cypriots losing their lives and nine others being seriously injured.

Between the 1 April 1955, when the EOKA struggle commenced, and the 30 March 1959, when the fighting stopped, a total of five hundred and nine Greek, Turkish, and British people lost their lives, and one thousand two hundred and fifty-eight were wounded.

***

In the Central Prison in Nicosia is a small cemetery called the *'Imprisoned Graves'* where the bodies of thirteen EOKA fighters are buried. Nine of them were hanged by the British, three were killed during clashes with security forces, and one died in hospital from wounds which occurred during fighting.

To save space the men were buried two to a grave without a priest or any members of the family present. The British Administration wanted to ensure that there would be no opportunities for mass demonstrations or protests at funerals.

***

In November 2014 a memorial was unveiled and dedicated in the English Cemetery in Kyrenia.

It is described as a *'triptych'* and bears tribute to the Greek, Turkish, Maltese, Maronite, and British police officers of the British Colonial Police in Cyprus, who lost their lives during the struggle with EOKA, as well as officers of the United Kingdom Police Unit seconded to the island who also died during the violence. The names of eighteen British officers are listed, together with forty-four from the other nationalities. The location is within the 'occupied' area and as such no member of the British Government was present at the opening ceremony.

***

Nicosia is the capital of Cyprus and is roughly in the centre of the island. It is much drier and hotter in the summer than on the coast where residents benefit greatly from a sea breeze. Its history can be traced back to the Bronze Age and it became the capital in the 11th century.

The Lusignans transformed it into a city, building a royal palace and over fifty churches.

In the 16th century the Venetians built 4.5 km of city walls, which encircle the whole of the *'Old City',* and have eleven heart-shaped bastions and three gates built into them.

***

(Andry):

"My sister Eirini (Roulla) was born in Nicosia on the 17 October 1958.

When she was just a baby the troubles were going on with the British as members of EOKA fought with British soldiers, demanding that Cyprus become independent.

One day something had happened locally and British soldiers came to search my parents' home. My mother was in bed with Roulla so they didn't disturb her but my father was arrested and taken to a prison.

My mother tried to go on a bicycle to see him and had Maro on the back. She started riding through the fields outside Kioneli village, which was quite a distance from Kaimakli where they were staying.

On the way she bumped into my grandfather Takis, who was travelling from Paphos to Nicosia in his lorry. He stopped to speak to her and passed by my mother's home later on the way back. He was always trying to see her and my two sisters whenever he could.

My mother took a short-cut, to save time, through an area that was forbidden to use, and she almost got shot by British soldiers but when they saw the child they didn't.

Kioneli is also known by the name *'Gonyeli'* and was a Turkish farming community, near to Nicosia. It is now in the 'occupied areas'.

The prison was a building with a high wall around it, and when she got to the front gate she asked to see him and they brought him there to speak to her.

At the end of the visit my father gave her a letter to give to someone. My mother couldn't read but she asked someone else to read it to her and then realised that the letter was to a girlfriend, so it was never delivered.

My mother was very disappointed and upset about this but she loved my father and had children with him so wouldn't leave him.

Whilst my father was in prison my grandfather brought food for my mother and looked after the family until my father was released.

Obviously he was questioned on suspicion of being involved in troubles against the British but they had no evidence and finally let him go.

My parents had a big argument about the letter and things got worse when my mother later found another letter in his pockets to a girlfriend.

My grandfather cautioned my father to behave but he didn't so finally he came and took my mother and the two children back to Paphos.

Eventually my father went to my grandfather's where he apologised and took the family back to Nicosia."

***

(Andry):

"My sister Chrystalla was born on the 12 January 1960 in Nicosia.

Whilst my mother was pregnant with Chrystalla there was a discussion with my father about giving their next child for an adoption to close family friends that were not blessed with children themselves.

My mother had doubts but my father was keener on the idea as he was worrying about how to care for three children. At the time they didn't know if it was going to be a boy or a girl so the agreement was that if it was a girl they would give her away, but if it was a boy they would keep the child.

My mother gave birth at home as somehow this was a rule from the hospital. It was a different experience for my father as he witnessed, for the first time, the difficulty of giving birth.

A midwife was called when my mother started to have pains and the minute my mother held her new-born baby girl in her arms she made her decision final. Chrystalla was not going anywhere away from her. No more adoption discussions – she wasn't giving away her baby.

On the 2 February 1961 my mother gave birth to another baby girl named Ioanna, which in English is the equivalent of the name Joanna. My mother said that she was a very pretty girl, like an angel, with white skin and very long eye-lashes. She was a big baby, and looked about three months old rather than just new-born. She was a very easy baby and my mother was very sure that she was going to grow well with no difficulties.

Unfortunately when she was just nineteen days old Ioanna caught a cold infection from my sisters. My mother took her to the doctors and he gave her an injection but the medicine was too much for her – she died in the early hours of the same day.

My family held a short ceremony of some sort. They held her in the air and classed it as a baptism saying words to the effect of *'In the name of the Father, the Son, and the Holy Spirit we baptise you'*. Ioanna had not been properly baptised at that point and unless you are a Christian the priests do not like to bury you in the Greek Orthodox Cemetery, so they had to do something to be able to do this."

***

(Andry):

"Life was tough for both of my parents. My father tried to work and support the family and my mother stayed home to look after the children.

I think my father found it more difficult to adjust to his role as a father, and a husband, as he married very young and had no other experiences with other women.

My mother was also young and inexperienced but somehow she had a very strong motherhood feeling and was very dedicated and caring for her children.

My father, at some weak point in his life, ran away with a nurse, I think it was around 1963 according to what my mother said, and this woman was from Varosia.

At the time my mother was left with Maro, Roulla, and Chrystalla to look after.

My mother reported the matter to the English authorities and somehow he was traced in England where he was working. The first salary he got was taken away from him and sent to my mother. He was told that if he didn't return that the money he got there would be sent to her.

In the meantime my grandfather took our family back to Geroskipou to look after them. When my father came back he went there and my grandfather found him a job."

Figure 4 Loukia - Andry's mother before her marriage. (Pre-

1956)

Figure 5 Group picture - the wedding of Andry's parents in

August 1956

Figure 6 Andry's parents – Costas & Loukia on the day of their

wedding in August 1956

Figure 7 Loukia - Andry's mother (Post 1956)

Figure 8 Costas - Andry's father (Post 1956)

Figure 9 Antigoni & Christodoulos - the parents of Andry's

mother in later life

Figure 10 Irinou - the mother of Andry's father in later life

Figure 11 Aristotelis - the brother of Andry's mother in his

30s/40s

Chapter One

1965

The Birth

Paphos is known as the birthplace of Aphrodite and is a coastal town in the southwest of Cyprus. There is archaeological evidence to suggest that the town existed in Neolithic times, and there are many historical sites dating back to ancient Greek and Roman periods, when it was the islands capital.

Paphos is famous for its castle, which was built as a Byzantine Fort by the Lusignans in the 13th century to protect the harbour. It was dismantled by the Venetians in 1570 and then rebuilt by the Ottomans after they captured the island in the 16th century.

Today a pelican that wanders freely amongst the many tourists and locals, and the castle, serve as a backcloth to 'open air' music events, such as opera and the theatre.

Old Paphos, which was otherwise known as Kato Paphos, has in recent years become home to many retired English people.

The Akamas Peninsula is the island's largest nature reserve, stretching from Paphos town all the way to the top of the island towards Polis.

Geroskipou is a coastal village to the east of Paphos and is one of the largest municipality's in the Paphos District. It is known as a village *'blessed with water'*. It borders the sea to the south and has a water dam in the north fed by the river Amathos, which comes down from the Troodos Mountains.

It is known locally for the production of *'Cyprus Delight'* or *'Loukoumia'* which is a sweet confection made of jelly, almonds, sugar, starch, and sprinkled with icing sugar, using a recipe which is more than one hundred years old.

The name of the village stands for *'Holy Garden'* and in Greek mythology it was the site of the goddess Aphrodite's sacred gardens where olive and carob trees were plentiful.

In more recent times a British Company set up a factory in the village in 1925 and hundreds of local people were employed there until it closed in 1952.

In 1960 Geroskipou had a population of just 1,727.

The village was once home to the British Vice-Consul Andreas Zimboulakis who was born in Kefalonia in Greece, before settling in the village. His former home is now a Folk Art Museum.

***

(Andry):

"I was born at midnight on the 5 November the 1965 in Paphos General Hospital before going home to a house we rented in Geroskipou – my mother says that it was an easy birth!

In actual fact my mother says that on the hospital records they showed that I was born at 11.55pm so that it counted as a day and she was allowed to go home a day earlier. In those days they kept you in hospital for three or four days.

They have a saying about the children of midnight, 'If you are born at midnight the darkness is covering you and people don't know what you are doing – *'pedi tou mesaniktou'*.

At the hospital the nurse who was looking after my mother saw my father visiting her and asked her if he was her husband. She said that she was and the nurse said that my father had been flirting with her and her sister at the same time – my father obviously was never giving up!

My mother already had three girls, Maro aged eight years, Roulla aged seven years, and Chrystalla who was nearly six years of age.

She wanted to have a boy, and she had prayed to God. In our religion we tend to dedicate our unborn babies to a named saint. I was dedicated to Saint Andrew, the first student who followed Jesus. If I had been a boy I would have been named Andreas, but after being born a girl my mother gave me the name Androulla.

I don't know if my parents were disappointed to have another girl but I do know that I was loved a lot as a new-born baby and I had all the attention of my parents.

It did however lead to a great sense of jealousy from my third sister, who felt that I had taken her place in the heart of my parents. In the years to come we had lots of fights and some aggression between us. Now it is something for us to both laugh about!

My mother used to say to me what a delicate, and tiny, baby I was, and that everything I wore looked perfect on me. Some of the neighbours that had a baby at the same time as my mother kept talking about me and comparing!!

My sister Maro recalls that on the second day after coming home my mother was accidently injured.

She had prepared a little plastic baby bath in the kitchen and after bathing me she had asked Maro to mop the floor as it was wet. In an effort to do the whole area Maro moved the chair that my mother was intending to sit down.

As my mother went to sit, with me in her arms, she dropped sharply onto the floor.

She didn't let go of me but suffered for a month after as she had hurt the last bone at the bottom of her spine and couldn't sit down properly because of the pain. My mother shouted at Maro who ran and hid until she had calmed down.

In accordance with one of the customs my nails and hair were not cut until after the christening because it was considered not to be good as I wasn't yet a Christian. A child not yet christened is considered to be vulnerable to evil it has to have a little gold cross, in order to protect it, plus a little icon of Santa Maria – the mother of Jesus. They also put them in the corner of the cot to keep it safe when a child was sleeping.

In our religion a baby that has not yet been christened is vulnerable to evil forces and should always be in the company of a Christian to protect the child.

Maro remembers that I was quite a dark-coloured baby and my mother was dressing me in what they call *'mesorropouthkia'* which are pure white cotton baby-suits that roll around the baby, including the arms, and hands so that they don't move. This was considered to be good for a new-born child to keep them warm and help with colic and belly pains.

On another occasion Maro recalls that one day my mother washed and ironed all of my clothes and placed them on a big black armchair before putting them away.

Maro had a cat called *'Prizou'* that was pregnant and unfortunately just at this moment the cat lay on the clothes and gave birth to her kittens!

My mother went furious when she saw what had happened. She picked up all the kittens and threw them down the hole of the toilet outside.

Maro says that it took her a long time to use the toilet again as she imagined that she could hear the kittens crying, and the poor cat was crying looking for her kittens for days.

Obviously Maro was only eight years of age and there was nothing to be said to my mother.

***

Maro also remembers a very tragic story at around this time, which relates to the loss of her godparents.

One day at the village of Kythrea, where her godparents lived, a charity event was taking place on behalf of a co-villager who was in great need. Maro's godfather had the need to have a pee so he stepped over to a ditch. As he was standing on the edge of the ditch he slipped down and called out for help. His best friend ran over but as he tried to reach him a rock fell down and hit Maro's godfather on the head, and he died on the spot.

Nobody could believe what had happened and, all the village was devastated at the loss of a young person in this way. Maro recalls that his mother was so upset that she pulled all of her hair from her head.

His wife refused to go out of her house for a long time and she grew hair on her face. They also had two young children as well. At some point she was taken to Germany for treatment after getting sick through her bereavement.

Unfortunately this proved not to be the end of the story as years later the sister of Maro's godmother persuaded her one day to join her on a trip to Kyrenia. Despite rarely leaving the house she agreed to do so but on the way they had an accident in their car, which crashed down some very steep cliffs, and they were all killed.

The two children were orphaned and grew up with their grandparents.

***

During this first year my father was working as a driver loading ice into a lorry in Limassol and delivering it to Paphos."

Chapter Two

1966

The Christening

(Andry):

"I was christened in Agias Paraskevi in Geroskipou, Paphos. The rich people did big parties with lots of guests but my mother doesn't remember us having a party, and in accordance with the custom then she stayed at home.

The church of Saint Paraskevi is one of the oldest and most important churches in Cyprus and remains virtually intact.

It is in the form of a basilica with five domes, three larger ones over the central aisle, and two smaller ones in the middle of either of the side-aisles. This cross-shape style is in the same style as the basilicas of the Holy Apostles in Constantinople and of St. John in Ephesus.

Wall paintings have survived from different periods in the church and in some parts there are two layers of painting, some dating to the 8th, 9th, 10th, 12th, and 15th centuries. Murals include *'The Baptism', 'The Raising of Lazarus' 'The Dormition of Theotokos',* and the *'Last Supper,the Washing of the feet, the Betrayal, and Christ Helkomenos'.*"

***

(Andry):

"Religious icons are an important feature of Greek Orthodox churches and revered by members of congregations. It is normal for those who follow the Greek Orthodox faith to kiss the icons, on entering a church, which are mostly protected by glass covers.

Alternatively the icons are covered in gold or silver with just the face of the saint showing. There are usually a number of women who will look after the inside of the church and they will regularly clean the icons.

It is done to show respect to the saints and the church asks women not to wear lipstick so as not to get it onto the icon.

As you enter the church it is also normal practice to take two or three candles, make a small donation to the church, and then to light the candles in trays of sand, which are usually by the main entrance doors. Then you say a prayer and ask God to look after the people you love.

My godparents were friends of my fathers. They were both teachers and had a reputation for being tough with the money. People kept saying to my mother, *'Don't give the baby to them to be baptised because they won't give any presents to her after the ceremony. They baptise a lot of other children and after that they forget about them.'*

But obviously my parents were not taking into account what other people said, although more or less it was true. I saw them many years later on the day I got married and I didn't even recognise them. In between maybe they came to see me twice in all those years, but it doesn't matter really, although in Cyprus godparents are normally very involved throughout the life of a child particularly on birthdays and celebrations such as Christmas.

Being a godparent in Cyprus is normally taken very seriously. If anything happens to the parents they take over responsibility for the child above all. They are also supposed to teach the child about religion and to give guidance. The godparents pay for all of the clothing for the ceremony, the cost of the church, the little gifts to people and half the cost of the party afterwards. They also pay for a present for the mother and play a big part in the ceremony.

When the baby is baptised the priest crosses the child with the *'holy oil'*. This must stay on the child for three days. No shower, or bath, or any kisses or touching the skin of the child is allowed until the godfather or godmother gives it the first bath.

Whoever helps with dressing the child after a baptism has to wash their hands with soap in the same bath that the ceremony took place. That water must go into a deep hole that is especially made for this and is put into the churchyard, or somewhere that people cannot walk over it, as this would be considered to be a bad omen.

The same thing must be done with the water that the child has its first bath in after the christening, as well as the water used for washing all of the child's clothes worn for the last three days.

The purpose of all this is for the holy oil to be saved. Any nappies have to be burnt. Finally when this is all done a big dinner party with only close family is held to celebrate the new Christian Orthodox entering into the religion.

I am the godmother to my sister Despo's daughter Gavriella."

***

(Andry):

"My mother told me that she was breast-feeding me until I was fourteen months old. Then my mother became pregnant with my sister Despo so she needed to stop, but I refused. She tried different methods, like putting pepper on her nipples. Finally what put me off was black coloured shoe paint!

I was very upset but my father bought me a rocking horse to make up for it! My sister Maro remembers another story about toys.

My father went to Germany for his first operation on his spine and when he came back he brought with him three very big dolls, two with blond hair, and one with black.

My sisters Roulla and Chrystalla took the two blond ones and ran out to play with them. By the time they came back with them they had been half-destroyed. Maro kept the one with black hair safely in its box and when my grandfather Takis visited he said that if it was still in a perfect condition a year later he would give her one pound, which was a lot of money then.

When we moved the following year my grandfather came to visit us and sure enough Maro showed him the doll, which was still in perfect condition on top of a wardrobe. As promised she was given her pound which I think my mother had.

Unfortunately I saw the doll and insisted on having it. I cried and cried until my mother gave in and told Maro to give it to me. Within hours I had destroyed it!"

Figure 12 Agia Paraskevi Church in Geroskipou, Paphos

Figure 13 Agia Paraskevi Church in Geroskipou, Paphos

Chapter Three

1967

Famagusta & Another Sister

In the early 1970s Famagusta, which was also known as Varosia, was the number-one tourist destination in Cyprus with high-rise hotels, beaches, smart restaurants, and a thriving port. It was regularly visited by stars such as Richard Burton, Brigitte Bardot, and Elizabeth Taylor.

The area was known for its numerous groves of oranges and every year an *'Orange Festival'* took place with decorated floats and music.

At one time there was even a train running between Famagusta and Nicosia.

Following the Turkish Invasion of Cyprus on the 20 July 1974 the Greek Cypriot Army withdrew its forces to Larnaca, and the predominantly Greek Cypriot civilian population, numbering some 39,000 people, fled to other parts of Cyprus.

The term *'Varosha'* originates from the Turkish word *'varos'* meaning *'suburb'*. It is a district of Famagusta, in the southern section, and is a fifteen-minute walk from the walled city.

The Old City of Famagusta is enclosed by walls built by the Venetians. On the landward side a dry moat, sometimes 100 metres wide, runs outside the walls and on the seaward side the harbour is located.

Today it is commonly referred to as a *'Ghost Town'* where the only presence is the Turkish military and access is forbidden to the general public. Barbed wire and fences clearly indicate that this is a 'closed area' which for all intents and purposes has been lost in time.

***

(Andry):

"We moved to Varosia after my father got a job in the port. Some friends of my uncle Telos helped him to find it. This is a common practice in Cyprus where families and friends always look to support each other so if you have a relative who is a hairdresser that's where you get your hair done, if you have a friend who has a restaurant you would be expected to show support by eating there. You would of course also expect to be treated specially!

At Varosia my sisters Maro, Roulla and Chrystalla used to have to walk a long way to get to the school on foot and would be given *'sisitio'* at school – milk and a piece of bread. They didn't mind to walk though because there were lots of trees with flowers blooming in the summer on the way to school and near the church of Panagia Evangelistria there were some catacombs so it was an interesting walk.

My sister Roulla remembers these walks well and although they were just young children they felt totally safe.

My father bought a Vespa motorbike and on Sundays he used to put Roulla and Chrystalla in the front, with Maro on the back, to go to the beach.

***

My younger sister Despo, otherwise known as Despina, was born in Varosia on 2 August 1967.

In time this created challenges for the sleeping arrangements as I always liked to sleep next to my mother in bed, but as Despo grew older she wanted to occupy this place. We would fight and usually I won, at which point Despo would sleep at the bottom of the bed next to my mother's feet.

She got her name from my step-grandmother Despina, who had married my grandfather Chistodoulos after he divorced. I remember that Despina had a big round sink made from marble in the garden of her house, which was quite unusual. She also had lots of flowers, and a huge fig- tree in the middle of the garden, as well as some other trees.

Under the fig tree a big 'swinging cot was hung from the biggest branches. This was very attractive to us, especially me and Despo, and we liked to play in it when we visited.

Despina also had a big fire-oven for baking bread, or cooking food.

The toilet was in the corner of the garden, like a stone building with just a hole in the ground. I used to hate to use it as it was very smelly and I was scared that I would fall in!

This was the normal toilet for all houses at the time.

***

We used to visit my father's father in Kythrea. He had a house next to the mountain, and next to the house was his sheep-fold with a stream running next to it. Then there was the toilet in a little shed with just a hole in the floor.

Houses were mostly built of a mixture of clay bars and hay. There was no cement. The walls would be about two feet thick. On the roof they would put wood and cover it with a *'plithary'* of hay, mud, and clay. Outside they would make the walls white with asbestos. The windows were wooden so that if they were closed you would not be able to see inside. The water had to be boiled and there would be a shower.

My grandfather Christos was brought up by an uncle here and his job was to look after the sheep fold.

Cypriot families were suffering from poverty and my grandfather's family was one of the many. So as a child he needed to work in order to support himself. So he moved in with his uncle and it gave him work and support by giving him food and shelter.

My grandparent's home consisted of two long rooms, with a kitchen, and storeroom at one end. My grandmother's bed at the other end of the room was very old and high with curtains all the way round. The four corners had like knobs on the end of the wood and sometimes we would unscrew them to play.

There was a big wooden hand-made mirror above the dressing table sculptured with vine leaves and sparrow-like birds. My sister Roulla was in love with that mirror and always she said that she wanted it after they died.

A very high wooden wardrobe covered the whole of one wall and on the bottom there was a row of big drawers. One drawer was always full of peanuts and other sweets kept there for us when we were visiting.

That said my grandparents did not show much affection to us and were not smiling people, but we still loved them and we also wanted to visit for the nuts and sweets!

Sometimes they were giving us *'one grosi'* which today would be about fifty pence. The value of money at the time was much different and worth much more. But I do remember the later years after my brother was born that my grandfather was giving my brother Michalis a five shillings note because he was a boy. It was a sort of discrimination between boys and girls where the boys were obviously more valued.

Now after the occupation their home has been demolished, and all of their belongings have gone. Now only some chickens live there. When the crossing points were opened in 2004 to allow people to visit the North I went with my father to visit the house and was shocked by what I saw.

There was nothing to show that once a lovely little home was built there and people had family and had a history there."

***

In 1967 inter-communal clashes continued to take place, and after previous problems in 1963 the village of Kophinou, a Turkish Cypriot village situated half-way along the main road connecting

Nicosia and Limassol, and Limassol and Larnaca, was defended by armed Turkish fighters. Nearby was the Turkish Cypriot village of Mari, and then a mixed-village called Ayios Theodoros.

Tensions increased in October in the area as Greek Cypriot police patrols were prevented from visiting Ayios Theodoros, and in the middle of November 1967 clashes occurred when units of the National Guard surrounded all three villages. In the fighting that followed twenty- four Turkish Cypriots and two Greek Cypriots were killed.

Figure 14 Andry on a rocking horse (circa 1967)

Figure 15 Andry (centre) with sisters – Chrystalla/Maro/Roulla

(circa 1967)

Figure 16 Andry (circa 1967)

Figure 17 Famagusta (Varosia) before 1974

Chapter Four

1968

Agios Nicolaos

Limassol is the second largest town after Nicosia, and sits between the ancient cities of Amathus and to the west the kingdom of ancient Kourion, founded by the Ageans in the 13th century BC.

Towards the end of the 7th century AD the Old Limassol was established and it eventually became known as Lemesos or Limassol.

Limassol has mile after mile of sand and shingle beaches and a 14th Century Castle which dominates the Old Port area. It was built on the site of an earlier Byzantine castle and is where *'Richard the Lionheart'* is said to have married Berengaria of Navarre, in the Chapel of St George, on the 12th May 1191, and where she was crowned Queen of England.

The story goes that Richard I, who was better known by the above name, took part in the Third Crusade to free the Holy Land.

The Crusaders fleet carrying Berengaria, and his sister Joan, was forced to put into Limassol for shelter due to severe storms, and Richard's ship arrived shortly afterwards on the 6th May 1191.

Richard became involved in a confrontation with the island's ruler Isaac Comnenos and succeeded in ousting him, before assuming ownership.

Richard the Lionheart later sold the Island to the Knight Templars, for 100,000 *'byzants'* gold coins.

They then resold it to another French Crusader, the nobleman Guy de Lusignan, the deposed King of Jerusalem, in 1192.

The Great Mosque was also built in Limassol on the site of another church, during the Ottoman rule.

After the invasion in 1974 the town received a substantial influx of refugees from the occupied parts of Cyprus, and the town grew together with an urgent need for additional homes.

Limassol was also the town where Vassilis Michaelides, the national poet of Cyprus, lived and died, was the first town to have telephones, and the site of the first power station on the island.

Today a brand new Marina provides a lifestyle for some of the more rich and famous.

***

Around 1968 the family moved again – this time to Limassol.

(Andry):

"The name Agios Nicolaos is Greek for *'Saint Nicholas'*. A number of villages in Greece and Cyprus bear this name but this was an area that we moved to in Limassol.

Just before we moved to Agios Nicolaos my father bought an old car so we could go to different places. My grandfather Takis was always asking him to move closer to where he lived because he missed seeing his grandchildren but it was not meant to be.

When we moved there our rented home was a small house next to a dry riverbed. I don't remember if there was any running water in the winter months but I do remember that we could pass through and into some fields on the other side with grass and plants for the animal food.

We were only poor people, so almost all of our clothing and shoes were handed down to us by other families.

The house was not big enough really for a family of seven but we managed somehow.

At the time it was not very inhabited but there was a big church of Ayios Nicolaos situated by the main road of Grivas Digenis, a street named after the leader of EOKA. There is a big cemetery next to it. The hiding place of Grivas Digenis in Limassol is further down the road and is a place that all schools are visiting, as well as tourists.

We would never go hungry; my mother was always making sure that she was feeding us well. We always ate first and she was always eating what we were leaving on our plates as she didn't like to waste anything. It was a loving time for us as kids in that we were not realising the reality of our situation. Of course above all is health, which we were fortunate to have.

My mother used to like to make marmalade at a certain season, mostly summer as it passed into autumn. She made it with some kind of yellow berries when they were ready to be picked. The trees were growing wild in the fields normally by the mountains. A drive out of Limassol was enough to find these trees and we would collect them either by hand, or by placing a big old sheet round the tree and then shaking it with our hands, or with big long sticks so that all of the *'mosfila'* would fall down.

My mother used to fill up a big aluminium kind of container with them. I think it was the one she was using to wash our clothes in, as we didn't have a washing machine for years.

I loved that marmalade! I also liked concentrated milk on a piece of bread, or sugar on a piece of bread. We had margarine, which was in a yellow and blue labelled tin called *'Blue Band',* and we used to spread it on a piece of bread with sugar.

That was our *'chocolate'* or our sweet when we were hungry between our meals.

My grandfather Christodoulos, 'Takis', visited us regularly and was always bringing lots of shopping. With so many people in the house, and only my father working, at times it was difficult.

The life at Agios Nicolaos however was for me as a child lovely with no worries, lots of adventures and peaceful. We played all day and explored.

***

I believe that it was towards the end of 1968 that my mother had another problem with my father again. He went abroad to have an operation on his spine in Germany.

When he came back he had like a cine-film, which he put on a projector. My mother saw that he had another woman with him and my father asked her to sign some papers to allow her to come and visit him. They had a big argument and my father took his clothes and for a while slept in his car by the beach.

Whilst he was away my grandfather from Geroskipou brought food to our house.

You might wonder why my mother put up with my father's behaviour in relation to other women over the years. It has always been clear to me that my father did love my mother and I suspect that he has never lost his feelings for her.

However Cyprus was, and still very much is a male-dominated society where if a married man takes a girlfriend he gets a slap on the back from his friends – like a 'well done', and is accepted with no rejection. However if you are a married woman, and you take a boyfriend, you are regarded as a whore and rejected for your behaviour by the family.

Some years ago I was told a funny story which I am sure has a lot of truth to it, and illustrates what goes on sometimes.

'This married man was dressing up in his hunting clothes at the weekend and telling his wife that he was going to hunt birds. A lot of people go hunting in Cyprus so this is quite normal. In the boot of his car though he had another set of clothes and after he left the house he used to get changed and visit the 'cabaret clubs' in Limassol where he used to meet up with other women for paid sex. At the end of the night he used to buy some shooting game birds from a friend, and get changed back into his hunting clothes before going home. He thought he was being very clever.

What he didn't realise though was that as soon as he left the house, his wife was phoning her boyfriend to come round to visit her.

They used to tie a rope to the balcony of the bedroom at the back of the house so that if the husband was coming back early the boyfriend could escape – who was fooling who!'

***

In 1968 Glafkos Clerides and Rauf Denktash engaged in bi-communal negotiations in an effort to resolve problems between the Greek and Turkish Cypriot communities.

Figure 18 Andry – front centre – Koulis and Christakis to the

right at back – 1968

Chapter Five

1969

Holy Days & Holidays

(Andry):

"I was born into a world where life was, and still is, hugely influenced by a calendar of yearly events, some of which are driven by religion, some by politics, whilst others are simply about being a Cypriot. All of them are important, particularly to family life, and they are embraced by communities – large and small alike:

On the 1 January (New Year's Day) we celebrate *'Protochronia'* and wish everybody a Happy New Year – by saying *'Kali Chronia'*.

***

The 6 January is known as *'Epiphany'* – *'Fota'* is the 12th day after Christmas and is known as *'Ta Fota'*, which means the light. On this

106

date big celebrations take place in harbours around Cyprus to celebrate the baptism of Christ.

A bishop or priest leads a procession to the water's edge where they throw a ceremonial cross into the sea to bless the waters. Local men then dive into the water to retrieve it and whoever does so is said to be assured of good luck for the rest of the year. Older Cypriots who tend the land will wash fruit and vegetables in the blessed seawater to try to ensure that they have good crops in the autumn.

***

An annual event to mark the beginning of Lent takes place in February in Limassol with the coming of the carnival – fifty days before the Greek Orthodox Easter.

It starts on a Thursday, which is called *'Tsiknopempti'* when everyone lights the charcoal to cook meat, and sausages, and the smoke gets everywhere.

'Tsiknopempti' means *'Stinky Thursday'* a name attributed to the smell of cooking meat in the streets. As you pass houses you can

see families gathered with the *'foukou'* or barbeque in full swing and tables laid outside for the food to be eaten.

The first week of the carnival is called *'The Meat Week'* – *'Kreatini'*, whilst the second week is called *'The Cheese Week'* – *'Tyrini'* which is when dairy products are eaten.

Food that might be consumed during this period could include ravioli, patties, the *'kaloirka'*, which is similar to ravioli but with mincemeat, various pastries and meat dishes like the *'daktila'*, the *'titsiries'*, the *'pishies'*, the *'tisiropittes'*, hand-made pasta, sausages, and pilau rice with oatmeal. This is to start getting into the fasting period gradually.

The first Sunday after *'tsiknopempti'* a big children's carnival takes place near to the coastal road in Limassol.

A further grand parade normally takes place in Makarios Avenue, where anything up to 50,000 people can be in attendance, with up to one hundred and fifty floats taking part, led by a Carnival King or Queen.

As young children we used to dress up in the village and go door-to-door where we would be given sweets.

The tradition of the Carnival – *'Apokries'* can be traced back to Pagan rituals, and is chronicled in mediaeval times, under the Franks and Venetians. It was specifically commented upon in 1566 by someone on their way to the Holy Land, who witnessed these events on the island.

It was more evident in Cyprus in the 19th century under British rule when all households, rich and poor, threw their doors open to people in masks and costumes. People would gather in groups and make their way to town squares where they would listen to music and play pranks on each other.

At this time serenading *'kantada'* started where three or four singers would support someone playing a guitar or a mandolin.

One of the most popular areas for this was at the Old Port area near the castle where people dressed up in gold coloured costumes.

***

The day after the carnival finishes is called *'Green Monday'* or *'Kathara Deftera'* and is very family focused.

It marks the official start of the fifty days of Lent which ends at midnight on Easter Saturday. It signifies the leaving of sinful attitudes behind, as well as non-fasting foods, and the start of preparations for cleanliness both spiritually and externally. The idea is that you head towards Easter with a clear conscience, a sense of forgiveness and renewed Christian love.

On this date, families head for the countryside or open spaces, with picnics made up of vegetarian food. Many people also take kites with them to fly and the emphasis is very much about spending time with the family and being outside in the fresh air at the beginning of the spring season.

Prior to Green Monday a lot of food preparations take place, for example: *'Houmous'* is a very popular dip that is made from chic-peas, tahini, lemon juice, garlic and olive oil. The chic-peas must be soaked in water for twenty-four hours before being boiled in water to make them soft. They are then blended and mixed with tahini and then the other ingredients are added. Cumin is a spice that will give a special taste to the *'houmous'* and it is then ready.

'Taramosalata' is popular as well, and is a fish-based dip.

Lots of vegetables are washed and dried including cabbage, lettuce, cucumbers, and tomatoes.

Green and black olives are prepared, as well as *'tsakkistes'* which are cracked green olives soaked in olive oil, lemon juice, garlic cloves and dry coriander seeds.

We also boil potatoes for this day and beetroot is a must. Above all, *'halvas',* which is made with tahini and comes with different tastes like vanilla, almond nuts, peanuts, pistachio nuts or coffee flavour. It is something that you buy ready-made.

'Laganes' are bought last on the Monday morning as they are made in the bakeries, soft and hot for the day. This is a specific kind of bread with sesame seeds on the top and very tasty.

On this day we are allowed to eat fish which has no blood in it, such as squid, prawns, or octopus accompanied by the rest of the food, and cooked on charcoal.

***

The 25 March is Greek Independence Day, which is a national holiday in Greece and embraced by Cyprus. It is both a religious holiday celebrating The Annunciation to the Virgin Mary, and a national holiday honouring the 1821 Greek Revolution against the Turks. On this date a national military parade takes place, with lots of flag waving in evidence.

It is also normal practice for the schoolchildren to have their own marches waving both the Greek and Cypriot flags.

***

The Easter *'Pascha'* is very important in the Cypriot calendar. The Lenten fast is observed by Cypriots of all ages, in varying forms. It is a very strict one and for those that observe it fully it prohibits meat, fish and dairy products, and even olive oil in the final Holy Week of the fast.

In some shops the word *'nistisimo'* will appear on signs indicating whether the food is suitable for fasting.

During the Holy Week there are daily church services at sunset when a special anthem to *'Our Lady'* called *'Hairetismoi'* is sung.

Everyone cleans the house ready for Easter and early on Good Friday the custom is for *'flaounes'* to be made. These are special Easter cheese pies flavoured with sultanas and mint, according to everyone's taste. They are beautiful to eat but can be heavy on the stomach!

Later in the day women go to the church with armfuls of white, and cream coloured, flowers. Inside the church they decorate the *'Epitaphios',* a wooden tabernacle.

After nightfall the *'Epitaphios'*, carrying an icon of Christ, is lifted onto the shoulders of men and taken around the village, or in towns, in a procession led by the priest, and escorted by children carrying candles. All the people attending the ceremony go underneath the icon being carried on the *'Epitaphios'* as it is carried from the church.

On Holy Saturday youngsters prepare a bonfire near to the church, which is lit in memory of Judas Iscariot and his betrayal of Christ.

At about 11.30pm everyone gathers for the Easter midnight service, carrying special Easter candles.

The priest *'Pater'* begins the service, with the churches always packed and the high point is at midnight.

As the clock strikes midnight the church is plunged into darkness. There is a brief silence and the priest proclaims *'Christos Anesti'* – Christ is risen, to which the congregation replies *'Alithos Anesti'* – he is truly risen.

The church bells ring and the priest lights the candles of all those around him. They in turn light the candles of those behind, and then they do the same to those behind them and so on.

Very soon the church is bathed in candlelight and everyone greets each other with the priest's words. It's really amazing how quickly all of the candles get lit.

Outside the bonfire is lit and fireworks are set off, whilst people try to protect the flame on their candle to keep it alight until they get it home. The custom is to keep it lit for forty days afterwards.

Nowadays some of the bonfires are huge and the lighting of the fire has lost its meaning as youngsters compete to set-off large 'bangers' and fireworks, in a process known as *'Lambratzia'*.

It is not uncommon for accidents to occur and for people to sustain injury as illegally manufactured bangers are lit, and in the days before the police frequently seize large quantities of fireworks. Sometimes young people even fight over the wood for their bonfire as they vie to build the biggest.

***

The 1 May is *'May Day'* – *'Protomagia'* or Labour Day. To honour this day big paradestake place, usually in the big towns, involving Trade Union members.

To celebrate the spring, floral wreaths are hung outside the entrance doors to homes to ward off evil.

***

During August many Cypriots take their holidays. This is considered to be the hottest month of the year and all building construction stops for two to three weeks.

***

One of the biggest *'name-days'* occurs on the 15 August and celebrates the Assumption of the Virgin Mary. Most Cypriots have been named after a particular Saint, and likewise churches hold a *'panayiri'* festival when it is their *'name-day'*.

'Panigiri' or *'panayiri'* is a big market, with different types of stalls, and they sell all kinds of things from toys for the kids to kitchen and household pans, bedding and towels, to sweets. Traditional food is also available such as *'loukamades', 'pourekkia' 'pombes', 'vamkaki', 'koupes'* and lots of other things.

In the early years this was a good way to buy and sell goods, as there were no supermarkets, and very little transport.

***

At the end of August the Limassol Wine Festival takes place in the Municipal Gardens, in the town-centre. It has been going on since 1961 and is intended to promote Cyprus wines. We used to go as a family to the wine festival and have something to eat there like sardines, and sausages and kebab in pitta bread. My father used to get a bottle of wine as it was offered free.

There were lots of different kinds of stalls selling things like 'palouzes' and 'koupes' as well as 'loukoumades', which seemed to be everyone's favourite. That said no-one made 'koupes' better than my mother who always made them on our birthdays!

A big statue of 'Vrakas' is put at the entrance to the park, and my father once had a picture taken in front of it. The statue is of a traditionally dressed Cypriot and stands maybe ten to fifteen metres tall.

Similarly dressed dancers demonstrate their skills and everybody just enjoys the atmosphere.

At the open-air theatre inside the park a play would take place every night and demonstrations would take place showing the traditional way that wine was made. People were sometimes invited to join in and it was great fun to enter a big round barrel with bare feet, feeling the grapes squelch underneath as the juice ran into a big basket from a side tap.

The festival was very popular with people, particularly English visitors, because the wine was free. I remember that we saw a lot of people drunk there one year and many of them climbed into a pool of water near to the entrance and got very wet!

***

Throughout September the grapes are harvested, as well as carobs, which used to be known as *'the black gold of Cyprus'* due to their export value. In late September the village of Anoyira in particular holds a festival to celebrate their harvest.

There are also twenty villages around Limassol that are known for their wineries where tourists can visit and try free wine tasting. These villages include Agios Amurosios, Lofou, Vouni, Omodos, Vasa, Malia, Arsos, Pachna and Anogyra.

***

The 1 October is Cyprus Independence Day, and once again schoolchildren get involved in parades.

**

The 28 October is Greek National Day – which celebrates the *'Ohi'* with parades and dancing taking place. The day commemorates the famous negative reply by the Greek Prime Minister Metaxas to Mussolini in 1940 after the latter demanded the surrender of Greece during the Second World War.

**

The 30 November is the *'name-day'* for Saint Andrew, which is my own *'name-day'*.

There are lots of people with the name Andreas, or Androulla in Cyprus, in most families, and the day is celebrated a lot.

The day starts with a big ceremony at the church and a priest reads out the names of the people celebrating their name-day. At the end of the ceremony *'collifa'* is given out in the yard of the church and *'best wishes'* are exchanged in Greek – *'Xronia polla gia tin giorti sou – na ziziz'* – which means *'Many happy returns for your name day'*.

It is normal to either go out with friends and family for a meal or most common is to be home and to welcome friends and family with snacks and drinks, or even food. Visits can start from morning until late at night, as everyone has to visit and say *'Happy name-day'* and normally take flowers or a small gift with them.

'Andrew the Apostle' in the Greek Orthodox tradition is called *'Protokletos'* or the first- called Christian Apostle who was the elder brother of Saint Peter.

They were both fishermen by trade and were called together by Jesus to become disciples and *'Fishers of Men'*.

Saint Andrew was himself also eventually crucified in a very cruel manner on a side-wise positioned cross.

There are two important stories that are connected to Saint Andrew and Cyprus.

The first story is that a ship carrying Saint Andrew went off course and ran aground. When he came ashore in Cyprus Andrew struck the rocks with his staff and at that point a spring of healing waters gushed forth. The ship's captain was blind in one eye and when he took some of the water his sight was restored. Thereafter the site became a place of pilgrimage and a fortified monastery was built there in the 12th century. It was the place from which Isaac Comnenos negotiated his surrender to Richard the Lionheart.

The second story is that in 1895 the son of a woman called Maria Georgiou was kidnapped. Seventeen years later Saint Andrew appeared to her in a dream telling her to pray for her sons return to the monastery in Cyprus. Living in Anatolia she embarked on a crossing to Cyprus in a crowded boat. As she was telling her story to other passengers a Dervish priest overheard her and asked her if her son had any distinguishable marks on his body. As she explained that he had the priest removed some of his clothing and revealed the same marks. Thus mother and son were reunited.

Apostolos Andreas Monastery is dedicated to the memory of Saint Andrew and is situated just south of Cape Apostolos Andreas at the north-eastern point of the island on the Karpasia Peninsula. It is also known as the *'Lourdes of Cyprus'*.

It is served by a religious order of monks as well as groups of volunteer priests and is revered by both Greek and Turkish Cypriots as being a holy place.

As a child I visited the monastery before the invasion but it is now in the 'occupied areas'.

***

The 25 December is Christmas Day and although it is celebrated it is not as important as the New Year. Christmas cakes were brought to Cyprus at the end of the 19th century but the Cyprus version tastes very different as the fruit used is *'glyka tou koutaliou'* which is preserved fruits in syrup. The cake is also decorated with homemade marzipan.

We make our cakes this way so that they last longer before going off.

Cypriots like sweet things and my sister Despo is no exception. When she was two years old she remembers regularly visiting a small market near to where we lived.

She used to like the long black rubber sweets and she used to take one and hide it behind her back thinking that the shopkeeper hadn't seen her. The owner used to say 'Can you sing the song of the owl' which is called *'Kou Kou Va'*. You need both hands at the side of your mouth to do the song but obviously Despo could only do it with one hand! The owner used to think that it was very funny and would always give her another sweet."

Figure 19 At Agios Nicolaos –

Chrystalla/Andry/Christodoulos/Despo (circa 1969/70)

Figure 20 At Agios Nicolaos – Despo/Andry/Chrystalla (circa

1969/70)

Figure 21 Paphos area – Andry's parents (circa 1969/70)

Chapter Six

1970

The First Engagement

(Andry):

"When I was five-years old my mother used to take us to see my grandmother Antigoni at her house in Famagusta. The beach was just across the road from the house – clear shallow waters. After my grandmother Antigoni left my grandfather Christodoulos I think that she lived with someone else for a while, and eventually she remarried and finished up living in Greece.

My grandmother had a piano in one of the rooms and I used to go in and lift the lid up to try to play it. I just used to finish up pressing lots of the keys at the same time and made a lot of noise - I don't think that my grandmother was very pleased! The piano was used by one of her sons, my uncle Kakos, who I wasn't very familiar with at that point.

We also used to visit my grandfather Christodoulos (Takis) and he used to buy us new shoes for Christmas and Easter. Because we were a poor family there was no money for toys, so it was always shoes or clothes that other families were giving to us. He used to take us to the shop of his nephew in Paphos called *'Margaritis'* and we would spend time making sure that they fitted properly. It was like a special occasion.

Our grandfather was always joking with us when he was 'farting' while he was walking or sitting in his armchair. He would try to say that it was his shoe that was making a noise but we would laugh at him and insist that it was him, *'farting'* – it was great fun.

I remember him carrying one of us on his shoulders, whilst another of my sisters was holding onto one of his legs so he carried both of us."

***

(Andry):

"I was maybe five years old and I remember an incident which I always called *'the great escape'*. It was on one of the days that we didn't go to the kiosk and all the kids from the neighbourhood were playing at the back of my home in the fields.

We got across the dry river and as we looked in the distance we could see the sea. Someone asked whether we should go to the beach; and we all agreed. So suddenly we all started walking towards the sea. I was still only five years old and Christos was a year older than me. My younger sister was aged three, Lakis was maybe seven years of age, and I don't remember who else was with us.

We walked quite a distance and we were determined to reach our destination. We knew the way there because we were going almost every day with mum to the kiosk. Not a busy area, actually more or less everyone knew everyone there.

At some point we passed through a home for elderly people. Someone spotted us walking without being accompanied by an adult and came after us. It was a deaf person and he realised that we had left home on our own. With his stick pointed towards us he started yelling at us to turn back, and made us walk back home. He wasn't able to speak properly and I remember I was very scared of him.

When we reached my house I ran and hid under the bed. But my mother thanked him for his help and for bringing us back home safely. At that time I didn't understand that he was a good person with what he did. At that time I was upset with him for what he did but I was just a child.

I think I showed from those years that I was a bit different and although a scary child I was looking for adventures – I felt different."

(Andry):

"My sister Maro was just thirteen and a half when she started having a relationship with a boy called Kokos, who was aged sixteen at the time.

She met him on the beach by the kiosk on the 1 August 1970 and remembers that she was impressed by his acrobatic and climbing skills in the nearby trees.

She plucked up the courage to draw a map showing where we lived and leaving it under a bottle so that he could find it.

We were still living in Agios Nicolaos at the time and after that Kokos started passing by our house, on his small bike, and on school days he used to ride alongside Maro as she rode her bicycle there.

Maro also used to go to cut a carob tree to feed my mother's goat and would take the chance to meet him.

Kokos had been coming and singing outside our house and initially my father had thought that he was singing for my mother!

Then Kokos had an accident and he was a patient in Nicosia General Hospital. My sister went to see him with the sister of Kokos. My father followed them and he saw her kiss Kokos and realized that they were having an affair.

Maro remembers that she was very naïve at the time and wanted to get engaged just to get to eat some chocolates! She knew nothing at all about sex and laughs when she recalls that initially she wouldn't let Kokos kiss her because she thought that she might get pregnant.

My father was very strict with us and if anything sexy came on the television he would send us to bed straight away. There was a film actress at the time called Zoe Laskari who used to show her legs and if she came on the TV that was it – we were not allowed to watch.

***

We were always getting into scrapes and Despo recalls that this year we visited Nisi beach near Agia Napa. Roulla and Maro were swimming in deep water and Despo wanted to go to them. I gave her a bamboo stick thinking that it would help her float, but the minute she started swimming she sank under the water and she remembers me pulling her out with the stick."

Figure 22 At Agios Nicolaos – Andry's mother with

Christodoulos (circa 1970)

Figure 23 At Agios Nicolaos – The birthday of Roulla –

Maro/Despo/Andry's mother/Roulla/A friend Garifallo (which

means 'carnation' in English) Andry/Chrystalla (circa 1970)

Chapter Seven

1971

Living On The Beach

Andry):

"On the 1 January 1971 the family of Kokos came to our house and the families agreed on an engagement. Instead of saying that she was too young my father agreed to engage her on the same night. She was under-age and any arrangements needed to be signed for by the parents.

On the 21 February 1971 a big party was held at my parents' house to celebrate the engagement. It was raining heavily so they placed the tables underneath the roof of a partially constructed house next door.

The priest who came to bless the engagement took out his books and was asking them to give him details of the *'prika'* so that he could write down the details. This was to be the agreement between the two families about what land, house, kitchen-wear or bedding was to be given to the groom. This was the custom.

Maro recalls that her future father-in-law told the priest that there was nothing to write down in his book – whatever each family could give they would give. Therefore no formal arrangement was made.

I don't remember much of my sister's engagement but I do remember the lovely *'kourapiedes'* that we offered at her party.

Just after the engagement I was eating one of these delights – a *'kourapies'* in the yard of our house. We had two turkeys and one of them jumped on me. I fell on the ground by the fence and my jumper got stuck on it. I couldn't stand up and the turkey jumped on me and grabbed my delight and was eating it. They must have heard me shouting and screaming and my family came to rescue me but I was still crying as the turkey ate my sweet and I didn't stop until they gave me another one.

One thing that my sister Maro remembers however is that on the day of their engagement a *'kokoromachies'* or hen-fight took place, which was one of Kokos's hobbies.

He used to breed a specific type of bird called *'gypsies'* which had long necks, and were very colourful. It was fashionable in those times and people were betting lots of money on the outcomes of fights, although Maro doesn't recall Kokos betting.

I seem to recall seeing one of these fights which was vile and quite frightening as the birds fought to the death.

Maro moved to the house of Kokos and the school turned a blind-eye to let her carry on with her studies although it was actually against the rules for engaged girls to stay on.

Kokos had agreed to let her stay on at school but once she moved he stopped her from going.

In accordance with the wishes of Takis, our grandfather, Maro always kept her hair, which was naturally black, long and straight."

***

On the evening of 31 August 1971 General George Grivas landed secretly in Cyprus, from a boat near Pissouri, and was taken to a hiding place in Limassol, being the home of Diana Mavros, who acted as his secretary.

He moved between this address and the home of Marios and Elli Christodoulidou, which was also in Limassol.

In September Grivas launched the new underground organisation known as *'EOKA-B'* whose stated aims were to oppose the 'pro-independence' line adopted by the Cyprus Government, to overthrow Makarios, and to proclaim Enosis.

The stage was set for further violence, and political instability, which would eventually climax in events that would fundamentally impact on the history of Cyprus.

***

(Andry):

"I remember on one occasion that me and my younger sister Despo, and our friends Christos and Lakis, were looking in the dustbins and rubbish bags for nice things that we could use, mostly I would say for broken toys. We were fascinated to see if we could turn somebody else's rubbish into something useful.

***

These were the best years ever spent by the beach where my mother was renting a little kiosk, in the summer months when the school was closed, or at the weekends.

Our normal routine was either to walk, or for my father to drop us at the kiosk, before he drove to work. It wasn't far at all from where we were living at the time. So, my mother every morning was getting ready for the day at the beach. She was, and still is, in love with the sea!

So the first thing to do on our arrival there was for her as quickly as possible do the cleaning, inside and outside of the kiosk, and then to jump into the chilly sea-waters without any hesitation. She would swim for a good half-an-hour and then that was it. The rest of the day she was the perfect businesswoman and the mum to have an eye on us all day.

Life by the beach was lovely. We had no worries. We all tried to help my mother with running the place, so first thing in the morning, by 7 or 8 o'clock, our job was to clean the beach of any rubbish and to 'comb' it with a special rake so as to make sure that there was no broken glass or anything dangerous hidden underneath the sand.

Then we went over the sitting area with a brush and took away all the leaves which had fallen from the huge eucalyptus trees which gave us generous shade. Then we sprayed the whole area with seawater so that all the dust settled. After this we cleaned the tables and put the ashtrays back on them.

Once the doors of the kiosk were open all the stuff needed to be placed just outside. Different stands with crisps and sweets had to be filled and sorted. We put the kettle on for hot water for the coffees; and the fridge had to be filled up with soft drinks. A small cooking appliance was placed in the corner as well for my mum to cook lunch. She was always preparing cooked food in the best way ever, tasty and delicious for all the family to be fed as well!

We used to regularly eat *'kolokasi'* which is a big root plant which is toxic until cooked. It is usually planted in March and harvested in October and the plants need a lot of water. Normally you fry large chunks of it with chopped onions and celery before adding puree and salt and pepper. You simmer it until the *'kolokasi'* goes soft then serve it with fresh bread.

We also had *'fasolaki'* which are long green beans, made in the summer when beans and tomatoes are at their best. You can add potatoes to it and the cooking technique is called *'yiachni'* which means stew.

My mother also used to make *'koupepia'* which are stuffed vine leaves with rice and mince. The leaves are washed in warm water to clean them to make them soft. They go a darker green in the water. You put olive oil in a pan and lightly cook minced onion, before adding minced pork normally, and lightly cooking again.

Then you add rice, pepper, parsley, mint and tomato sauce. After this you add one teaspoon of the filling to each leaf and wrap them. Then they are put into a pot with water and lemon juice before cooking for about thirty minutes. They are delicious!

Another of our favourites was called *'faki'* which is lentil soup. It is first cooked in a *'presto'* and chopped fried onions are added with *'fide'* or rice. To create a better taste my mother was also adding chopped carrots and tomatoes with olive oil.

We used to sleep under very high eucalyptus trees – the shade underneath was perfect. My mum had a camp bed that she made for us to have a siesta between 1pm to 4pm when the sun was burning and it was too hot to be in. We used to sleep with the sound of the *'tzitzikes'* crickets, and the noise of the trees as the wind was blowing among them.

Always there was a nice warm food ready by one o'clock and then we had to have a nap till four o'clock. This was a must and my mother would not accept any arguments. As children we just wanted to play, and play, but my mother wouldn't accept any disagreements. We had to sleep and rest, and then again until late afternoon, until it was time for us to go home. In between we were playing on the beach, and helping a little bit with serving soft drinks or coffees.

On one occasion my mother had put us to sleep and there was this man sitting by the kiosk. Whilst he was watching us he was playing with his private parts. I remember that I was scared and embarrassed so I covered myself under the sheets and pretended I wasn't looking. But still I was curious and every now and then I would take a quick look to see what he was doing and if he had stopped or gone! Once again I didn't understand the dangers of what I was facing and was not educated about such things.

Sometimes the sea was bringing out big pieces of wood that had been floating in the water. These were our ships and we used to climb on them on the beach and pretend to be pirates.

Of course during the time we had the kiosk by the sea my mother could earn good money and she tried to save some, so I would say that we ate better during that period.

'Pappous' or grandfather was also always bringing us lots of bananas to the house, which were still not ready to eat. My mother used to place them in a black rubbish bag in a dark place, which was under the bed normally, so that they would get yellow and ripe. Every day I used to sneak under the bed very carefully, so that no-one would see me, and check to see if any of the bananas were soft enough and if so I was eating it quietly. Once they were all ready, from what was left my mum was hanging them from the ceiling somehow, so that we wouldn't be able to reach them.

Even so I would place a chair underneath and would do a big jump to get to the bananas like a monkey, grab one and go. Nothing could stop me from having one!

Even today I can't pass a day without a banana."

(Andry):

"In September I started school. It was all new for me. But I was a bit relaxed because my best- friend Christos was also going to be with me.

Christos was the brother of Kokos and I got on well with him.

Agios Nicolaos Elementary school looked huge to me. I don't have many memories of the place but I definitely remember that my class was on the second floor. On the first day in the class the teacher placed us into pairs, a boy with a girl. I wanted to sit with Christos but no, some other boy was put next to me and I was very upset.

I sat at the end of the desk as far as I could just in case this boy touched me. The time for a break sounded and we needed to hold hands with the next one to go down the stairs. I refused!! No way would I hold this boys hand. I didn't like him at all - I liked only Christos.

The teacher finally had to give up after failing to put me into some order and I won!! I was holding the hand of Christos to walk down the stairs - It was awesome!

***

I remember I had two English friends, Amanda and Julie, who were our neighbours at Agios Nicolaos. They lived in a house with big gates nearby with their parents.

Julie was the eldest, and Amanda was younger than me. Julie had blond hair with blue eyes and Amanda had ginger hair and lots of freckles. They didn't look like sisters. They didn't speak Greek and we didn't speak English but the language was not a barrier or a problem for us. We actually enjoyed trying to communicate with body language! It was a good fun.

They taught my younger sister and I how to ride a bicycle. We didn't have our own bikes so we were trying to learn on theirs.

To turn the wheel wasn't easy at all for me - once as I was cycling I ended up in the bushes on the rocky beach, but nothing could stop me from trying. I was a tough girl and never gave up until I learnt.

Once when Amanda and Julie were away my sister Despo remembers that she climbed over their wall to *'borrow'* their bicycles to play with.

***

Life was all about play. Once we set up a trap, me, Despo, Christos and Lakis. It was very popular to play with our *'billies'* (marbles), little round glass balls in two or three different sizes. So the plan was for us to steal a big bucket of them from another boy who was passing from our house.

We agreed that the strongest from us was going to push the boy on the ground and the others would pick the bucket up as fast as they could and run and hide. And so we did. We didn't care for what we were doing but only to collect more and more *'billies'* – the poor boy he just started crying and ran away!

We used to play between us by putting them in a row in pairs and then stroking them with our fingers, the middle one and the thumb, so our *'billia'* could hit the opposite sides and we were winning it. The bigger ones had a greater value.

'Ligri' was another game we used to play. We placed two columns of stones and a stick on top of them connecting them. Then with a big stick we hit the smaller stick in the air to send it as far as possible. Then we had to hit it from the ground and continued until we reached another set of stones set up at the other end. We were allowed to try only three times and we used to say as we were hitting the stick *'Matsa, Thkiotsa, Tritsa'* which means more or less *'Once, Twice, Three times'*.

Another game we used to like to play was called *'Skala'*. We drew with a piece of chalk on the cement floor or put sticks on the floor to make two square boxes. We then attached to it one square, then put another two boxes, then once again one, and then two more.

We would give a number from one to eight and then by using a flat stone place it on the first square. We would then jump with both, or one leg, all the way up and down the squares, pick the stone up and jump out. It wasn't so easy because on the single squares we had to stand on one foot only and keep our balance whilst at the same time picking up the stone. Falling meant we lost and nobody wanted to lose – we wanted to win!

Another cheeky play with my friends was to make holes in the ground and fill them up with water. We would then cover the holes with grass and pieces of wood. Then we would blindfold one of us and leave them to walk around until they fell into one of the holes. The fun was to fall in and get your shoes wet.

On another occasion I remember that I jumped into the hay storehouse, at our home, from the top of the roof. We were playing *'hide and seek'* and I thought that it was a perfect place to hide. As I jumped inside I was fully covered by hay and I felt like I was being suffocated. I believe I hadn't realised the danger of what I had done. I couldn't breathe. I rolled down off the pile and tried to get out of the storehouse through the high iron door. I struggled with it as the handle was very high and stiff to open. I had to call for help and after a while someone opened it for me. I never did it again as I was so scared.

Further down from our house another couple lived. The woman's name was Zooula and I think at the beginning when we moved there she had no children. She got one the year after and I remember that she had such a passion for cleanliness that she wouldn't let the baby out of its chair so as not to make a mess!

One day I saw a man walking in the bed of the river. He was finding toilet paper and eating it. I was so shocked. Zooula asked him to go with her so that she could give him food but he refused.

We used to collect crickets *'tzinzkikes'* in the dry river and tie them together with a piece of cotton on their legs or around their bodies. Then we would watch them fly around. If they were still alive we would let them go after. One day by mistake I collected black cockroaches instead. I can't bear them and they scared me!

As a child I had a lot of fears, I had a fear of heights, of the dark, a fear of being alone in the house and a fear of noises. I was scared of cockroaches, bats, needles, and injections. Overall although I was daring to do challenging things and was quite bold and strong physically I was something of a *'scary child'*.

I remember that my mother was told of a lady that could *'blow away my fears'* reading me some kind of spell and then giving me a little silver unshaped item to keep under my pillow for a month.

I don't know whether it worked or not because I lost the silver piece soon after being given it and the fears didn't go away until I became a mother!

At some stage my mother decided to have our ears pierced. It was going to be really painful but if we wanted to have earrings and look pretty we had to tolerate it. So one day she took us to this lady to pierce our ears. She was only using a needle and cotton. After I saw her doing this to my sister I refused to have it done at that time. Eventually my mother threatened me that if I said no again she wouldn't take me back. So I had to manage. I did cry and scream from pain but I guess it was worth it after all!

As for heights I am still scared but manage somehow to control it.

***

One day we were at the beach and I saw this man lying down. He was so white that I thought he was dead and I ran screaming to my mother to tell her that there was a dead man. She ran with me to where he was and then suddenly he moved!

At the kiosk we had no proper toilet so we had to go under a bridge nearby. It wasn't nice to go to the toilet there. It was smelling and full of dirt but we had no option. Always we would go in pairs so one would watch to see if anyone was coming. Thank god in the winter water ran under the bridge and swept everything away!

The kiosk was not ours. It belonged to the father of Kokos. His name was Costas Kokkinoforos and he had a much bigger kiosk two hundred meters from us. His kiosk was very popular and they were offering souvlaki and calamari. Ours was a very small kiosk and we were not allowed to offer any food except snacks, soft drinks etc. We were paying rent to them.

I remember sometime after my elder sister Maro got engaged to Kokos that there was an argument between the families and Kokos stopped Maro from coming to see us.

I was missing her so much that I used to go halfway to their kiosk and cry and try to see her. I think at the end I went all the way there and my sister came towards me and we managed to see each other. She was my favourite sister, and eight years older than me, and I looked up to her as a 'mother-figure' because lots of the time she had needed to look after us.

She moved to the house of Kokos at such a young age – it was all too soon but who was to know how things would turn out.

**

My sister Despo remembers that one night we were all at the kiosk waiting for my father to pick us up. It was getting dark and he didn't come. My mother was sat there with the five of us. Finally a woman that my mother knew took us to her house and we slept there for the night.

In the morning we went back to the kiosk and my father was waiting there. He said that he had been looking for us all night.

My parents had a big fight and my father abused my mother physically – he was late to pick us because he was seeing another woman.

***

After three years of living in Agios Nicolaos at we were about to move again to the place which finally became my home for many years – the village of Trachoni."

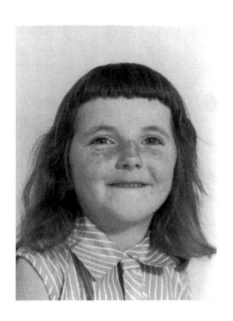

Figure 24 Amanda - Andry's friend (circa 1971)

Figure 25 Julie - Andry's friend (circa 1971)

Figure 26 Kyrenia – Andry's father/His Aunt Theodora and her husband. (circa 1971)

Figure 27 Kyrenia – A family gathering - Andry front row far right (circa 1971)

Figure 28 Famagusta – Antigoni & family gathering - Andry in middle of front row - (circa1971)

Figure 29 Agios Nicolaos – Chrystalla/Amanda holding a pigeon/Andry (circa 1971)

Figure 30 Outside the kiosk at Limassol – Andry on right (circa 1971)

Figure 31 Fighting Birds

Chapter Eight

1972

Trachoni Village

Trachoni is a large village, which lies in the Limassol District of Cyprus, on the Akrotiri Peninsula, with a large proportion of it being situated in the British Sovereign Base Area of Akrotiri.

Sometimes known as the Western Sovereign Base Area it includes the RAF base of Akrotiri, as well as the British Forces base at Episkopi, where the Commander of British Forces in Cyprus (CBF) is based. This position rotates between senior officers from either the Army or Royal Air Force.

Including Trachoni there are eleven village districts within WSBA which covers an area of nearly fifty square miles and is classed as a British Overseas Territory.

The area includes nearby beaches at Curium, and Ladies Mile, some of which are nesting sites for turtles, Limassol Salt Lake where thousands of flamingos gather every year, and also witnesses the annual migration of more than one hundred and fifty species of birds as Cyprus sits on a migration flight-path for millions of birds travelling between Africa and Europe.

The name of the village originates from the ancient Greek word *'trachon'* which meant rugged and stony ground.

The village existed under the same name in medieval times, and on old maps which have been found it is marked as *'Tracon'*.

The name of the village indicates that it is older than the medieval Frank era, and was most likely established during the Byzantine years.

De Masse Latri mentions the village as being a *'feud'* belonging to the Order of the Knights Templar during the 13th century. After the break-up of this Order it came under the protection of the Order of St. John of Jerusalem.

In the centre of the village is the Greek Orthodox Agios Mamantos Church, (New) and there is a much smaller Church of Agios Mamas (Old).

There are also three chapels, the Chapel of Agios Georgios, the Chapel of Panagia Chrysospiliotissa, and the Chapel of Panagia Katoklisiotissa – which is actually inside a cave.

Prior to 1974 Trachoni was inhabited by both Greek and Turkish Cypriots, although the Turkish Cypriots were in the minority.

The Turkish Cypriots called the village by the name of *'Kaykale'* meaning *'stone-made fortress'*.

In 1881 the population of Trachoni was recorded as 165 persons, in 1891 as 183 persons, in 1901 as 205 persons, in 1911 as 239 persons, in 1921 as 175 persons, in 1931 as 145 persons (106 Greek-Cypriots and 39 Turkish-Cypriots), in 1946 as 248 persons (186 Greek-Cypriots and 62 Turkish-Cypriots), and in 1960 there were 305 Greek-Cypriots and 117 Turkish-Cypriots.

After 1964, due to inter-communal clashes, most of the Turkish-Cypriots in the village left to re-locate to villages where they were in greater numbers.

Following the invasion in 1974 the few remaining Turkish-Cypriots left for the north.

In 1976 there were six hundred and nine Greek-Cypriots living in Trachoni, and the area subsequently received a large number of dislodged Greek-Cypriots when four Refugee 'self- help' housing settlements were created, and 543 new building plots designated in that area.

By 1982, as a result of this resettlement numbers in the village increased dramatically to 1,766.

Citrus, olives, vines, vegetables, cereals and fruit trees, mainly figs, are cultivated in the area.

In Cyprus local Community Councils are led by elected 'muhktars' or community leaders, who have quite a lot of power and influence over what gets done and when.

The 'muhktar' for Trachoni village between 1964 and 1983 was Demetris Lambrou who was very well respected for his leadership and was also the secretary of the Cooperative Bank for many years, as well as the Cooperative Supermarket, which was set up to try to help the poorer people in the village who had to manage with very little money.

In those days we still had the Cyprus Pound with lots of notes of different denominations with the lowest one being a five-shilling note. We also had small coins called *'Grossia'* or *'mpakkires'*

I remember Mr. Lambrou being a nice quiet man, and very much a normal person, despite his position of authority. He was married and I think he has two sons, and a daughter whose name is Koulla. She had a shop under her house and we used to buy clothing from her."

***

(Andry):

"After moving to Trachoni my parents carried on with the kiosk for a while, in the summer. My parents also had the coffee-place called *'Constantinos and Evripidis Football Club'* in Trachoni Village – it was named after two friends from Trachoni. One day they were going to Nicosia for some reason in the winter of 1963 and they disappeared and have never been seen again since.

Rumour has it that the two boys were killed by extreme *'facist'* Turkish Cypriots and thrown down a well but this has never been proved.

Members of the two boy's families still live in Trachoni to this day and there is a painting of them hanging on one of the walls in the coffee shop."

***

In November 1963 Archbishop Makarios submitted his proposals, by way of a thirteen-point plan, to amend the Constitution, and there was a lot of tension and a political crisis unfolded. At the end of December 1963 there was inter-communal fighting in Nicosia, and Nikos Sampson was involved with other Greek Cypriots in fighting with Turkish Cypriots in the area of Omorphita. Some Turkish Cypriot women and children were taken hostage.

A photo exists which shows him waving a pistol, and holding up a Turkish flag seized during the fighting.

Turkey threatened to invade Cyprus, and Russia threatened them that if they did so they would bring troops to Cyprus as well.

There was a lot of fighting between Greek and Turkish Cypriots in the area of Kofinou village, which is on the way to Nicosia, and people were killed.

***

(Andry):

"I remember that when I used to play with the neighbourhood children people were always throwing cigarettes on the floor of the coffee-place so I used to pick them up and go behind the chicken-house at my home to smoke them with the twins Christofis and Savis Thrasivoulou. Their father later became the muhktar.

This was an exciting thing to do at seven years of age!

My mother was the only woman in the coffee shop. She was always busy making lots of coffees on a plate, which had sand on it, for the men and boys who gathered there to talk about football, politics or to gossip about what was going on in the village. They also used to play a card game called *'Pilotta'* or *'Tavli'* which was a board game using black and white pieces.

The men get very excited when they are playing and it becomes very competitive.

Among the sweets that my mother was selling there were some kind of *'afroza'*, a white sugar dust that was fizzy when put in the mouth and was contained in something like the shape of a small ice-cream cup.

In some of these cups was a lottery ticket with a winning prize. Me being cheeky I used to open each one carefully, empty out the sugar, check to see if the lottery ticket was inside, and then put back the sugar and close the cup again carefully. I was doing this until I found the winning lottery and got the prize, which normally was a cheap toy.

On one occasion I was with a neighbour Costas Patakos, who was about the same age as me, and I was climbing one of the almond trees next to my house to get some of the almonds. He prodded one of the branches at the top and when I stood on it the branch gave way and I fell onto the ground. Costas was frightened, left me on my own, and ran away to his house. I fractured my right elbow which was put in plaster for a month which was good because I didn't have to do any writing at school.

Close to our rented house in the Old Village of Trachoni was the school and opposite was the coffee shop.

At the front of our rented home in Trachoni I used to cultivate small tomatoes and every day I used to collect them and eat them – maybe fifteen at a time.

Kokos used to have his fighting birds in the back garden of our house after we moved to Trachoni. I think at that point they moved in with us for a while and then something went wrong. There was an argument with my parents and they moved out again.

Opposite the house was a big tree in some fields with berries on called *'conafkia'* which I used to eat after they fell onto the ground.

At my school they used to tease me because they said that I was speaking in a posh voice. They were bullying me but I never let them get the better of me and I wasn't afraid of anyone.

Whilst I was at this school I met Anthoulla Agathogleous, who became a very close- friend.

***

In 1972 I went to my first funeral, at the age of seven years.

In Cyprus funerals are always very emotional and break the hearts of everyone that attends. My parents didn't normally allow me to go to funerals but this one was a child from the village just about three or four years old. He died from anaemia. In those days it was not always possible to keep people suffering with *'mesogiaki'* anaemia alive. These days' people can live quite a normal life with this condition.

It's something that many people from countries around the Mediterranean have. You can be a carrier of the anaemia, which is called a *'stigma'* or you can be more seriously ill whereby you need to clean your blood with a dialysis machine every night, and a blood transfusion every couple of weeks.

As a carrier there is no problem to your health as long as you take iron supplement for all of your life. The body doesn't absorb iron through food so it needs to be taken in the form of tablets or liquids. Without it you feel low, dizzy, and lack energy. It affects the hair, skin and nails which don't grow, and they become thin and brittle.

The dead child's name was Nectarios and he was the third child of the family, if I remember well. His sister Argyroulla was the same age as me and we went to school together. There was another brother Pambos who was a bit younger than I was.

I remember that there were so many people at the funeral, all crying and all wearing black. The child was carried, wrapped in a white sheet. I remember the child's face very clearly as looking very pale, as I saw it after they placed him in the grave, very deep.

It is customary to ring the bells in the church to indicate to everyone that a death has taken place in the community.

When people are buried in a coffin it is normal in our religion, after the service, to leave the lid of the coffin open when being placed into the grave. We say it helps the body to go into the ground quicker. Everyone has to take some soil and throw it into the grave. They say it is about letting go. We also throw in oil and wheat. It can get very crowded at the graveside as the grave is filled in with people standing everywhere, crying and screaming, and climbing over the soil.

I was so scared that I ran away and for three days I couldn't eat. I had the feeling that the smell of the soil in the cemetery was in my mouth and I couldn't forget the pale yellow colour of the dead child. I was terrified. Everything was having the same smell.

I was really upset for a long time and don't remember going to another funeral until I was fifteen years of age, when three schoolgirls lost their lives in a coach crash.

***

I remember a summer that we visited my mum's village, at Choulou, and we helped to collect the black, and white, village grapes from the vineyard of one of my mum's aunts.

I enjoyed it so much as the only thing I had to do was to ride the donkey and to try to stay on it between the two big baskets full of grapes. Someone was at the end of the vineyard to empty them.

All this was happening in August usually and it was very hot. We didn't mind as we were used to being under the sun with no hats and we had never even heard of sunblock cream in those days!

But the life in my mother's village was hard, simple but not easy at all. The people there were living on what they produced themselves such as from almond trees and olive trees, plus a little from a small market in the village. Every now and then they had to go to town to get necessities.

Many villages had no electricity and people used to preserve food in the fat of the pigs, or by making them dry exposed in the sun with lots of salt on. Very traditional were the sausages. Firstly they soaked small pieces of pork meat in a village red wine for eight to ten days. Then they got a whole pepper, mixed it with the pork a spice called *'ssinnos'*, and then stuffed the intestines of the animal to create the sausages. After this they would hang them in the sun to dry, or they were smoked to get the flavour.

Pasta and *'tsamarella'* was also very popular and when they had no meat they would mostly eat potatoes, beans, vegetables, fruits and nuts, and haloumi cheese.

***

In 1972 we visited Bellapais Abbey, Agios Ilarionas, before the invasion took place. It is near Kyrenia and was built as a house for Augustinian priests on the northern slope of Pentadactylos. The Abbey is now in the occupied areas.

When the invasion happened many of the residents of Kyrenia took shelter there. On one side there is a steep slope and I just couldn't look down – I was still trying to fight my fears!

Kyrenia is a town on the northern coast of Cyprus and is well-known for its castle and harbour. Centuries ago the population used to be fairly evenly split between Christians and Muslims but during the British rule it was inhabited mainly by Greek Cypriots. During this period they built a road through a mountain pass to connect Kyrenia to Nicosia.

It suffered from very little inter-communal violence but after the invasion nearly three thousand Greek Cypriots fled or were forced to leave. Today it is in the *occupied areas* and is populated by Turkish Cypriots, Turkish Settlers from the mainland, and some ex-pat British people who have bought property there.

In the same year we also paid a family visit to Apostolos Andreas Monastery near Varosia On the way we stopped for a swim at a beach. As we were all swimming suddenly my sister Despo fell down a deep hole in the sea and all we could see were her arms in the air. My mother ran to drag her out – Despo almost drowned.

Despo remembers being pre-occupied at the age of five years with dolls.

On one occasion, whilst I was at school, she played with my favourite doll. She used to like taking the head off and the arms and legs but whilst she was playing she lost one of the legs and when I got home I went furious at being left with a one-legged doll. I held her down and punched her. As I was older and stronger than her she couldn't defend herself!

On another occasion I turned the tables and offered to improve her Barbie doll, which had crazy hair all over the place and was dressed in old clothes. I made it beautiful and showed it to her but then refused to let her have it back.

Despo cried and eventually I decided to give it back to her but not before I had messed the hair up again and dressed it back in the old clothes!"

Figure 32 2nd grade Elementary School Trachoni Class Photo –

Andry middle row 3rd from left (circa 1972/3)

Figure 33 The old 'Agios Mamas' church in Trachoni Village

Figure 34 The new 'Agios Mamas' church in Trachoni Village

Figure 35 Coffee shop in Trachoni once run by Costas Christou

Figure 36 'Constantinos & Evripidis' – picture in Trachoni Coffee Shop

Figure 37 Kyrenia before 1974

Figure 38 1st Grade Elementary School Trachoni Class Photo –

Andry front row second from right – 1971/1972

Chapter Nine

1973

The Precious Boy Is Born

Andry remembers the moment that her parents received the news that would make them feel that their family was complete.

(Andry):

"On 21 June 1973 my brother Michalis was born.

Prior to that my mother had a very big gynaecological operation but without her knowing that she was already pregnant. They had difficulty waking her up from the anaesthetic after the operation and she also needed a blood transfusion. It was a very worrying time for all of us.

In Cyprus when relatives go into hospital it is not unusual for members of the family to spend a lot of time at their bedside for the duration of the stay. They always worry a lot and want to stay close.

My mother felt very uncomfortable when she realised that she was going to have another baby, as my elder sister Maro was already engaged to be married. It was kind of embarrassing for her.

But the doctor made it clear to her that she was having the baby by way of a caesarean. Doctor Koundouros was a very well known gynaecological doctor in Limassol General Hospital and knew my mother's family situation. He told my mother that she was having a boy and that he was going to be a teacher. He was right on the first count only.

We didn't have a boy in the family so that was a big surprise for all of us. During that period we still had the kiosk by the beach, so after a few days when my mother came out of the hospital, straight away she went back to work at the kiosk. I can't remember much about how my mother managed to be honest but I'm very sure that looking after a new-born baby, and all us, was a big thing. She never complained though – for her it was her duty to look after her family and she never put herself first.

Our time at the kiosk was the best of our lives with no worries, and lots of fun and play.

Sometimes I was forgetting to wear my swimming costume and I was ending to swim with only my underwear and topless. I remember that I was embarrassed and avoiding going close to people but it definitely didn't stop me from swimming.

My skin got very tanned and my hair went from black to blond from being exposed to the sun all day long.

When my brother was born my other grandmother Irinou, came to congratulate my mother by saying, *'God bless Stylianos – Na mas zisi'*, which is like many happy returns for this person.

My mum, with a big surprise on her face, tried to clarify who *'Stylianos'* was!

My grandmother insisted that the new baby boy was going to be called Stylianos as she had promised in church to Saint Stylianos, that their son would be named after the saint.

Saint Stylianos was born into a poor family in Adrianopolis, which is now part of Turkey, in the 6th century. In later life he sold all his worldly goods to give to the poor and lived the life of a hermit with just the clothes he stood up in.

He became the Patron Saint of Children, both born and unborn, and was said to have created a miracle by helping a women who could not bear children to conceive. He is said to have always had a smile on his face and religious icons show him holding an infant swaddling in his embrace to signify that he was the protector of children. His memory is celebrated every year on the 26 November.

Anyway my mother equally insisted that her son was going to be named after Papa Michaelis, her own grandfather, whom she loved deeply – it was going to be Michalis and that was it!

My grandmother was very cross with my mother but she was ignored by all of us and there were no more arguments on the subject.

At the same time my grandfather Christodoulos also tried to insist that the child be named after him and he also argued with my mother. But my mother refused to change her mind as she strongly believed that she owed it to her grandfather.

Michalis had his first swim in the sea from the second week of his birth and before he was forty days old he had been in the water at least eight times. I do remember that once he slipped from my mother's hands and suddenly he was under the water. That scared us all but baby was fine, thanks God!

My brother was growing strong and he was very healthy as long as we were by the sea.

As the winter came along he caught bronchitis and took a while to recover. I remember that my mother was every day placing him high on pillows with his head down lower, and she was tapping his back for the phlegm to come out.

***

There were always regular celebrations to get involved in as children.

Green Monday marks the beginning of Lent which is fifty days before Easter. Families always have a picnic in the countryside or in the back gardens. It consists of a meatless meal with lots of fresh vegetables.

My mother always fasted but as children we were expected to do it for just one week. We were too scared to cheat and ate beans, salads and fruits only. Anything that came from animals was prohibited.

The Greek Orthodox Church celebrates Good Friday with a symbolic enactment of Christ's death and burial.

After going to church, on the Saturday night, we would always go home and have a hot bowl of soup either *'trachanas'* or *'augolemoni'* and then bang boiled eggs together or *'tsoukrisma'* as we say in Greek.

It is still a tradition and whoever dents the shell of another's egg wins. The eggs are coloured red with some roots, beetroot boiled, or using some other natural colouring.

That's the end of the fasting period.

At Christmas we would go round in school uniform singing traditional songs called *'Kalanda'*. People used to give us sweets and money. We would have icing sugar-coated *'Kourabiedes'* almond flavoured cookies and *'melomakarona'* which were honey-flavoured semolina balls."

Figure 39 Agios Athanasios –

Roulla/Maro/Chrystalla/Despo/Andry – front row on right (circa

1973)

Figure 40 Trachoni – Roulla/Despo/Andry/Chrystalla (circa

1973)

Figure 41) 2nd Grade Elementary School Trachoni Class Photo

– Andry front row second from left - 1972/1973

Chapter Ten

1974

The Coup & The Invasion

On the 27 January 1974 General George Grivas died suddenly at the house of Marios Christodoulides in Limassol. Despite denials it would seem that he had been suffering from severe heart problems for some time, which at times had confined him to his bed. He was routinely referred to by many in EOKA-B as *'The Leader'*.

After the news broke, next day, thousands of his supporters gathered outside the house, to pay their respects.

Despite his opposition to the Cyprus government three days of national mourning were declared and his body lay in state, as he was declared to be a *'Worthy son of his motherland Cyprus'*.

The funeral of Grivas was held in an open area outside the house of Elli Christodoulidou in Limassol and was presided over by the dethroned Bishop of Paphos, after an offer to officiate by Makarios was refused.

Members of EOKA-B were present in uniform.

An impromptu speech was made to crowds of mourners by Nikos Sampson, following which he placed a copy of the newspaper 'Machi', of which he was the proprietor, in his coffin, which declared *'Thus the Great Field Marshal got to know in writing of his posthumous triumph'*.

Makarios ordered a general amnesty. Convicted and imprisoned EOKA-B members were released, and wanted EOKA-B members came out of hiding from the mountains, as it was hoped that the death would lead to an end to the violence.

The new leadership rejected the terms of the amnesty however, and on the 24 April 1974 masked EOKA-B men raided Pano Anglisides village, entering a café and houses, and ill-treating Makarios supporters, some of them in front of their children. The village priest was also beaten up and hit with chains. Before leaving they gathered in the village square, firing shots into the air. The following day the police recovered 1,000 spent bullet cartridge cases.

On the 25 April 1974 EOKA-B was declared an illegal organisation.

During a speech in June 1974 Makarios described it as a *'criminal syndicate'* and its former leader as having left Cyprus with a *'national scourge'*.

Even in death the fortunes of Grivas had again changed but the organisation he had spawned was determined to pursue its course.

Nikos Sampson, saw himself as the natural successor to Grivas, in the political pursuit of Enosis, although at that time was not officially connected to EOKA-B.

***

Heavy winter rains and snow brought an end to a long drought and in the spring of 1974 wild flowers created a blaze of colour, until the growing heat caused them to fade.

Elsewhere other *'storm clouds'* were gathering which would change the face of Cyprus forever.

(Andry):

***

"My sister Maro got married on the 5 May 1974 in a dress that was brought from England for her by her aunt Elou, and I was a bridesmaid. Kokos was not on speaking terms with some of our family at the time and Maro remembers that when she went to thank her aunt for the dress Kokos became violent towards her. It was not to be the last time.

Maro and Kokos received about three hundred Cyprus Pounds from the wedding guests but little did anyone know that this money would be needed to support the whole family when the coup took place."

***

On Monday 15 July 1974, at 8am, a coup d'état took place in Cyprus, based on a plan called *'Aphrodite 3'* as the code words *'Alexander has gone to hospital'* were issued. The operation had been ordered by the military Junta in Greece, staged by the Cyprus National Guard and supported by EOKA-B. It deposed the Cypriot President Archbishop Makarios III and installed pro-Enosis supporter Nikos Sampson as provisional President of a new *'Government of National Salvation'*, at 3pm that day.

The swearing-in ceremony was conducted by the dethroned Bishop of Paphos at the General Staff HQ.

The aim of the coup was the ultimate annexation of the island by Greece, and the *'Hellenic Republic of Cyprus'* was declared.

The head of the Greek Junta, Brigadier Ioannides, had believed that Makarios was no longer a true supporter of *'Enosis'* (union between Cyprus and Greece) and also suspected him of being a communist sympathiser, hence his support for EOKA-B, and the Cyprus National Guard, which at the time had some six hundred and fifty Greek officers within its ranks.

Just two weeks previously Archbishop Makarios had asked for these officers to be withdrawn from Cyprus. The response from the Junta was to order the coup to go ahead.

Makarios narrowly escaped death in the subsequent attack on the Presidential Palace, which began at 8.20am as tanks and army vehicles surrounded it. At that moment he was greeting thirty

Egyptian Sunday School children whom he had invited to Cyprus. The children were eventually led out of the Palace unharmed but some adults with them were treated roughly in the hands of their captors.

After initially seeking shelter Makarios managed to escape due to a series of events which he later described as a miracle.

After first going to Kykkos Monastery he made his way to Paphos, where he eventually went to St. Patricks Camp, on the town's outskirts, and was given shelter by Major Richard Macfarlane, Coldstream Guards, who was the Paphos District Commander for British Forces deployed there.

In the rush to escape Makarios was unable to put on his 'pendant cross' and had to borrow one from the Bishop of Paphos.

He was eventually picked up by a Whirlwind helicopter, which was deployed from RAF Akrotiri, and within fifteen minutes of landing there he was flown onto London.

***

Malcolm *'Doc'* Halliday is a retired Detective Sergeant with West Midlands Police, but at the time of the coup he was a corporal in the First Battalion of The Royal Scots, serving in Cyprus and based at Salamanca Barracks, in Episkopi, which was part of the Western Sovereign Base Area known as Akrotiri. This is his recollection of the early hours of the coup,

"We arrived in Cyprus in the spring of 1974 from the UK, having previously served in Northern Ireland. I was part of the Resident Infantry Battalion based at Episkopi and soon got used to early starts due to the heat.

As well as being a corporal I was also a piper and, as a member of the pipe-band, spent a lot of time doing parades. In our downtime we used to hire mini-mokes from the shops on the base at Episkopi and go exploring. We weren't allowed to go on the tourist beaches but we were soon introduced to 'traditional Greek mezes' and found the locals to be very welcoming.

Whilst many of us were living in barracks a lot of the married military personnel were actually living in rented homes in surrounding villages, and Limassol. These houses were called *'hirings'* and up to 10,000 service personnel, and their families, lived among Cypriot communities.

It was a similar story in Famagusta and Larnaca and they were known as *'dormitory'* towns.

When the coup got underway rumours were soon going around that Cypriots were fighting each other.

We needed to get the English families who were living in the *'hirings'* back to the safety of the Bases Areas and the idea was to open up safe corridors of some sort to Limassol and elsewhere. BFPS Radio had advised these families to stay indoors until help arrived. Some of the families we needed to evacuate lived in Trachoni village.

In Limassol there were a few confrontations with locals who at one point tried to disarm some British soldiers, sent in to evacuate people, but a couple of RAF planes flew overhead to discourage them. At the time some 'Lightning' aircraft were based at Akrotiri.

The town of Limassol had a population of about 31,000 Greek Cypriots, and 6,000 Turkish Cypriots, who lived in their own

Quarter, and things became very tense between the two communities.

I joined up with some soldiers who were sat in a Land Rover which had a trailer attached to it. Myself and another guy sat in the trailer which had a tarpaulin sheet over it. I had a look underneath and it was stacked with ammunition – not the best place to be if a stray bullet was to strike!

On that first day we went to the road known as the M1 and parked up at the T-junction. To the left at this junction the road heads off towards Kollosi Castle, whereas to the right it takes you to RAF Akrotiri.

There was some fighting going on in Kollosi and we could hear firing. I was told that some people in a bus were shot there.

People were driving by us in vehicles carrying very old weapons, shotguns, and howitzers, a rag-tag bundle of people.

It proved to be a long day."

***

In the book *'When The Tanks Started'*, which was written in Greek, the writers describe how a huge convoy of Makarios supporters left Paphos for Limassol on the day of the coup to try to help. On the way some elements of the convoy were told that there were people waiting at Kollosi, from the coup, to ambush them.

The main group then took another road, skirting the boundaries of the British bases, and entered Limassol via the Turkish quarter.

Not all of the convoy however received this information and a bus, with two vans, and a big lorry, containing about a hundred people were in fact ambushed at Kollosi, by the petrol station, and at the junction which leads to Akrotiri.

The Makarios supporters were in possession of a number of old weapons, and a couple of Bren guns, but were pinned down after stopping when they saw a man in Army uniform who they thought was a Makarios supporter.

Some hid in ditches as the firing intensified, whilst others were trapped in their vehicles. Four people died and around thirty people were wounded.

Following the fighting the coupists took about thirty prisoners to an Army camp in Polemedia.

***

At that stage the Turkish Cypriot community was not directly affected, and the Turkish Cypriot leader Rauf Denktash had referred to the coup as being an 'inter-Greek' event.

Paphos was initially the only town in Cyprus not to immediately fall into the hands of the forces supporting the coup and pro-Makarios townspeople organised themselves into a defensive force, as well as trying to help pro-Makarios supporters in Limassol. Columns of reinforcements, supporting the coup, then made their way to Paphos and the situation changed.

By the 16 July the whole of Cyprus was under the control of the coupists. During the course of the coup a total of five hundred and four people were killed and hundreds were wounded.

***

(Andry):

"We have a saying in Cyprus that something bad will happen when you hear an owl cry.

The night before the coup an owl sat on the fence at the front of our house and cried.

My mother looked very worried as this was a bad omen. She told us that something that was not good was going to happen and it did as the preparations for the coup were already underway and my father was not with us.

There was music on the radio, that morning, and suddenly it stopped and the coup was announced.

We were all scared worrying about what was going to happen next.

There were people in Trachoni Village who were members of EOKA-B and some people put sandbags on the roofs of their houses and sat there with guns.

My father was opposed to EOKA-B and went to a police station in Limassol to help. He was armed with a pistol. He was trapped there for a while, as it came under attack. Eventually he managed to get out smuggled in an ambulance which was driven by a friend of his, and had to pretend to be injured.

On the outskirts of Limassol my father was picked up by Kokos who drove him to Pedoulas village where he left him. From there he made his way on track roads through the mountains to reach Kykkos where he stayed until the invasion started.

Some of the villagers came to our house looking for my father and were asking where he was. They didn't hurt us but they were aggressive and we were very scared, although my sister Chrystalla remembers that she had a tape recorder which she tried to switch on to secretly record them!

They set a trap at the entrances to the village intending to shoot him if he came back.

My friend Alekos Constaninou remembers that his father was also a supporter of Makarios and likewise people from the village who supported EOKA-B came to search their home. The irony of the situation was that amongst them were some of their relatives.

Alekos has since forgiven them for their behaviour based on the fact that they were being influenced by people with other political beliefs – forgiven but difficult to forget.

At some point later my father came across one of the EOKA-B who was looking to kill him and as my father recalls he put the man on the ground, and pointed a gun at his head but then spared his life. I won't reveal his name though.

My brother-in-law remembers someone in the village being tortured by members of EOKA-B just because he was a socialist. It was a time of great fear.

On the day of the coup my sister Roulla remembers that she was at her sewing lessons in Limassol and because of what was happening it wasn't safe to collect her so she stayed the night with her teacher.

My school friend Anthoulla Agathogleous remembers that after the coup took place she and her father went to his sheepfold in Trachoni and found three police officers who had helped Makarios to escape to Paphos hiding there. They were very frightened and were trying to get back to Nicosia. Her father gave them food and tried to help.

We were scared as we were all females in the house, except for Michalis, who was just one year old. At some stage we all moved to my elder sister's Maro's home in Ayios Athanasios in order not to be alone.

My mother remembers that Kokos came in his car to pick us up, and as we were leaving we were stopped at a road block on the Limassol side of the village by EOKA-B supporters.

They searched everything in the car, even the tin of baby's milk for Michalis.

The nights were long and dark. We were not allowed to have any lights on because of the bombings plus we were sleeping outside on the veranda scared, in case the house was bombed, so we wouldn't be buried underneath. Also there just wasn't any room inside!

My sister Roulla recalls that it was very hot outside and the place was full of mosquitoes.

Despo remembers that she and I put a quilt in a tree over two branches and slept there for a while.

My sister Maro recalls that during our stay at her place we were eating lots of fish as Kokos used to fish using dynamite and caught lots in this way. He had a small boat and used to throw a stick of dynamite into the sea, which stunned the fish and they would float to the surface.

It was a dangerous practice though and the father of Kokos actually lost both of his hands in an accident with dynamite before we first met him. He used to hold a cigarette between the two stumps to light it.

At one stage he had things fitted to the stumps to help him hold things but he was getting aggressive and dangerous with them so they took them off him."

**

On the day of the coup Limassol's two police stations came under attack from National Guard forces and heavy fighting continued throughout the morning, as bands of armed EOKA-B and sympathisers roamed the streets firing weapons.

At the police stations four people were killed and three wounded during the fighting. As they were treated at Limassol Hospital, an urgent appeal was put out by hospital staff asking for blood donations.

In the book *'When The Tanks Started'*, the writers describe how thirty cars went to the Central Police Station carrying people from Paphos with guns taken from an army camp there.

There were people aged from fifteen to sixty-five years, and about two hundred in all, who were all Makarios supporters.

Among them were people wearing the traditional *'Vraka'* trousers and when one high- ranking police officer asked an old man why they were there he replied, 'We come to fight my son. We come to save Cyprus.'

***

Years later my father received a medal for bravery for his actions, and I am very proud of him.

His citation reads, *'The Committee of the Ministry with the decision of number 61.174 dated 16.11.2004 is awarded to Kosta Christou a medal of resistance in recognition of honour from the Cyprus Republic for his action of defending The Republic and the legacy for resisting to the Coup on the 15 July 1974 and defending the democratic elected President Archbishop Makarios',* signed by the then President of the Republic Tassos Papadopoulos.

He also received a commendation from a high-ranking officer in his command for his bravery as a volunteer soldier."

***

On the evening of the 15 July Turkey's National Security Council met to discuss the situation and their armed forces were put on alert. During the meeting discussions took place with regard to invoking Article 4 of the Treaty of Guarantee of the Constitution of the Republic of Cyprus.

Under this Article Britain, Greece and Turkey guaranteed the independence and the territorial integrity of Cyprus and had the right to intervene jointly, or if this was not possible, unilaterally with a view to restoring the status-quo that had resulted from the London-Zurich Agreements.

***

On Saturday 20 July 1974, at about 4.30am, Turkey commenced military action on the pretext of a peacekeeping operation, to protect Turkish Cypriots, in an operation codenamed *"Attila'*. Turkish ships approached the northern shores of the island, after a trip lasting some twenty hours.

In 1974 Turkey had the largest NATO army in Europe with some 453,000 men under arms, with modern equipment, much of which was of American origin. Some forty thousand Turkish troops took part in the operation with the 39th Division at the forefront, which had been formed in 1964.

The Cyprus National Guard on the other hand was equipped with aging weapons, many of which were of Russian origin, whilst others were remnants from World War II.

It had no Air Force, and a Navy armed with just five Russian-made torpedo boats.

At dawn on that date heavily-armed Turkish Forces landed at Kyrenia, on the northern coast of Cyprus, and captured 3% of the island, which included a narrow path between Kyrenia and Nicosia, before a ceasefire was declared on the 22 July 1974.

Also on the 20 July 1974 the inhabitants of the Turkish Cypriot enclave in Limassol surrendered to the Cyprus National Guard. According to eyewitness accounts large numbers of people were taken into custody, many of whom were taken to the main stadium in Limassol, following which parts of the Turkish quarter were burned.

West of Limassol the Turkish enclave at Avdimou was also surrounded by EOKA-B fighters and the occupants forcibly removed.

This particular confrontation was referred to in the book *'A Business of Some Heat'* in the following terms by a member of The Royal Scots, guarding the SBA entry points, *'A United Nations patrol under command of Sergeant Deakin (correct name actually Sergeant Deighan), Parachute Squadron, Royal Armoured Corps was sent to negotiate a truce with the Greeks. There then began a long period of negotiations during which Major Ashmore (Royal*

Scots Company Commander) was escorted to the Greek

positions...to arrange the truce. The escort consisted of a hard-line

EOKA terrorist in the back of the Landrover holding a grenade in

front of the car in which Major Ashmore was travelling!'.

***

Malcolm Halliday further recalls events,

"I remember I was woken from my bed, in the early hours, by someone asking for 'A' Company's piper, which was me at the time. I was half-asleep but was told to get my kit and my rifle and was simply told 'there's a war on' – I was somewhat bemused to say the least.

I decided to put my kilt on, and No 2 Dress uniform, which is a bit lighter to wear. I got my pipes, my boots, and my SLR rifle. Next thing I know I am priming phosphor grenades and full weaponry, before we made our way to the Kollosi T-junction to help with more evacuations from Limassol.

The Commander of British Forces Air Marshall Aiken had ordered the withdrawal of all British families into the Bases, and at 0530 hours that day the British Forces Broadcasting Service advised families to stay indoors and await instructions.

Other members of my Battalion supported RAF military police as they eventually gathered families together to take them in convoys to Akrotiri. As people waited in the heat fighting was going on in the Turkish Quarter.

Pregnant women were put into private cars, women and children in buses, and men onto trucks. They had very strict instructions to carry the bare minimum with them. One officer apparently tried to put his prize canaries onto a bus but was told in no uncertain terms that this was not allowed.

We also had the additional problem of trying to help holidaymakers from France, Germany, and Italy, who suddenly found themselves trapped in a war-zone.

To try to keep morale up I decided to stand at this junction and play the bagpipes as they started to bring families and holidaymakers back into the Bases. Some went straight to RAF

Akrotiri, to be flown of the country, whilst service personnel were taken to temporary accommodation.

I was just a young soldier and initially what I was doing didn't seem strange but as vehicles were passing people started banging on the sides shouting and encouraging me on. I had the biggest reaction from a load of fellow pipers in a four-ton lorry who were shouting and egging me on. It was like people felt safe as they heard the sound of the pipes.

In a subsequent issue of *'The Thistle'*, which is the Journal of The Royal Scots, I was quoted as saying *'They say the families were glad to see me, well I was more than glad to see them arrive safely, and I enjoyed playing for them all.'*

The story made some of the newspapers and I was referred to as the *'Piper of Cyprus'*.

Years later I was given a press-cutting which had appeared in a UK newspaper by one of the people who had been helped that day which sums it all up:

'*The road from Limassol to British bases at Episkopi and Akrotiri was choked with vehicles carrying servicemen's families and holidaymakers to safety. Shots had been heard, bairns were crying, mums worried, progress slow. Then the convoy heard the sound of the pipes. Piper Halliday of the Royal Scots in full highland dress was marching up and down, and everyone who heard his pipes knew they were safe. I wonder where Piper Halliday is now. To him it was probably just duty performed on a hot day, but we'll never forget him.*' (A.McCandish, Glenrothes)

It brought a lump to my throat.

At some point I was sent to RAF Troodos to give some advice and support on how to protect the site there and anti-riot techniques. From our position in the mountains we could see Turkish paratroopers landing and also Greek Cypriot tanks below us. Turkish troops were not far from our positions, indeed on one occasion I witnessed one of them shoot a stray dog with a shot from more than eight hundred yards away. He was clearly a good shot!"

***

David Woolmer was in the Royal Air Force at the time and recalls the following,

"In July 1973 I was posted to RAF Troodos as a Motor Transport (MT) Driver. My main duties were transporting staff to, and from, the radar sites on Mount Olympus and the *'hirings'* there being no actual married quarters and single-men's accommodation in Platres and RAF Troodos respectively.

I also did daily trips to RAF Akrotiri, as well as to Episkopi and Nicosia.

In March 1974 I returned to the UK to get married and returned with my wife to a fairly dilapidated but homely house in Platres which is still there to this date.

On 15 July 1974 the coup took place in Cyprus.

Wives and families were confined to their homes in Platres, and the husbands to RAF Troodos.

We still carried out regular trips up and down to Platres, via the Seven Sister's road, although we were now armed. We knew it was serious when we were issued with live ammunition and our yellow cards for firing instructions *'halt-stamata-dur'*.

As a driver my personal weapon was the Stirling Sub-Machine-Gun, surely one of the most dangerous weapons ever devised.

On one memorable occasion we were targeted by a rocket-firing Turkish Air Force F100. It transpired the actual target was a Cyprus Radio Mast a couple of hundred yards away.

On the 20 July the Turkish invasion took place and later that day an evacuation from Platres was undertaken.

I commandeered the Land Rover Field Ambulance and took my wife, a nurse, as passenger. We then picked up an assortment of lorries, cars, buses and taxis containing service dependents, tourists, some locals clutching old and battered British Passports and a party of Jewish tourists who seemed rather at home amongst the general confusion.

A fairly slow drive down the road to Ypsonas took place without any interruption. At the Ypsonas crossroads there were signs of a recent firefight, presumably between Pro and Anti- Makarios forces.

The convoy was then directed to drive to Episkopi rather than Akrotiri as Limassol married quarters were also being evacuated. The convoy ground to a halt somewhere outside Episkopi and this being the hottest day of the year it was somewhat uncomfortable especially when we heard a fairly heavy-machine-gun firing. After a few minutes the unmistakable sound of a Wessex Helicopter was heard overhead, a few rounds of a Bren gun and then silence.

We then arrived at Episkopi where billets were found and we reported to the Officer In Charge (OIC) of Motor Transport.

The Troodos drivers were now stuck in Episkopi as it was deemed too dangerous to return.

I ended up at Happy Valley Episkopi which had been turned into a tented refugee camp. These were all Turkish Cypriot civilians who were being turned on by the Greeks. A lot of the men were carrying weapons of various vintage with them and these were placed in the back of a three tonner lorry which I happened to be the driver of that day.

Information was received that a Greek National Guard unit somewhere up in the hills towards Paphos was holding some Turkish Cypriots hostage and would kill them unless the weaponry we had seized was turned over to them.

I think it was a Scots Battalion who, incidentally were on *'rest and recuperation'* from Northern Ireland, who came along as escort. An officer and three squaddies in a Land Rover and me, a Sergeant and four in the back of the open top *'Three Tonner'*.

On the drive to the village the four Jocks in the back started to make the weapons unserviceable. This including blocking the barrels on shotguns, rifles and pistols so that anyone attempting to fire on of these would certainly have been left with a serious headache.

By the time we got there it was now dusk and we were stopped by a bunch of National Guardsmen one of whom pointed a shotgun up my nose as I looked out of the cab.

He ordered the Landover to wait there whilst I followed a National Guard truck in the *'Three Tonner'* with the Scottish soldiers and the load of obsolete weaponry. After about three miles we stopped the lorry unloaded and about four or five Turkish civilians jumped into the back.

I then exited *'stage left'* at speed in the dark on dodgy mountain roads with the lights off. On arrival back to Episkopi I went for a cold shower and an even colder beer.

As things quietened down we were then allowed back to Platres and Troodos. The power in our house had been turned off and a piece of pork left in the fridge had become riddled with maggots and flies – I didn't eat pork for years!

We also found a note left by our landlord, handwritten *'British traitors' you belong in hell. Why don't you go back to your rotten country and stay there. Leave us in peace. If you come back you won't have life easy. This is not a threat but a promise.'*

He clearly felt a sense of grievance that Britain had not intervened militarily when the Turks invaded.

I kept the note as a memento.

A sort of normality resumed, but being forty miles away from the nearest Sovereign Base Area was always a concern and following the second phase of the Turkish invasion a full evacuation took place.

My wife went to Akrotiri and, despite trying very hard to stay, was flown back to RAF Lyneham in a C130 Hercules aircraft. As it was full of young children with their mothers she got a front seat for the eight-hour flight.

Back at Platres the married men were given about half an hour to pack a deep-sea box for sending back to the UK. I managed to fill ours with a few wedding presents, clothes etc. plus one or two bottles of NAAFI spirits, and that was it.

I then resumed duties at RAF Troodos for a further eight months before the end of my tour.

I had a Fiat Coupe, which I had got a mate to drive down to the SBA in the first evacuation. I met a Reuters Correspondent who was desperate for transport to cover the war. We reached an agreement and he paid me in US dollars.

Following the ceasefire, I went in convoy down to RAF Nicosia, now wearing UN berets and carrying UN stickers on our vehicles"

***

Malcolm Halliday continues his recollection,

"I came back to Episkopi and then got posted to Happy Valley, which is the SBA's main sports field complex. Initially we were instructed to block roads and not to accept any refugees. The Royal Engineers built big observations points made with sandbags, and with Union Jack flags flying openly from each one.

On the old road we set up a roadblock near to Avdimou, which is about 4km from Happy Valley. Opposite us was a Greek Cypriot machine-gun position and they occasionally fired over our heads.

We had armoured scout-cars with us to support us, as there were all sorts of people moving around with guns and in semi-uniforms. On some occasions we would escort them through the

Bases and on other occasions we would take their weapons from them and give them back after we escorted them from our areas.

On one occasion some Greek Cypriots came up to our roadblock with two trucks. In one truck were Turkish Cypriot men, and in the other Turkish Cypriot women and children. They were all clearly terrified.

I remember this one man in particular, who was about 5'4" tall, and wearing crossed bandoliers and carrying a big gun. He looked like a Mexican bandit. He was very aggressive and making demands to one of our officers which we could not quite fathom out. The officer sent him away and he left with the trucks. At that point the officer had specific instructions not to accept any refugees.

Shortly afterwards we heard firing and then the Greek Cypriot came back with just the one truck containing the Turkish Cypriot women and children.

Our officer immediately gave orders for them to be taken to Happy Valley but not before the Greek Cypriot asked for the truck back!

I can only speculate as to what happened to the men.

After this we started to take more Turkish refugees to Happy Valley where a tented camp was set up and eventually up to 5,000 Turkish Cypriots took refuge there from surrounding villages.

We were also involved in other evacuations as the troubles continued and were issued with yellow cards which gave instructions as to what to do when approached. We had to shout three times for people to stand still and use the words – *'Halt – Stamata – Dur'* – it could be very confusing."

***

(Andry):

"After the invasion began my father became a volunteer soldier. The duty to his country came first as he had strong beliefs about protecting Cyprus and his family. As he had been injured in the past, and had previously had the two operations on his spine, he could not be ordered to join the army. Because of his beliefs though he went as a volunteer and risked his life in an undercover operation against the Turkish troops.

Initially he formed a group of five persons and they were armed with a variety of old British weapons, including a Sten-Gun and a weapon made in Turkey. They used a Landrover to travel around, and after being at Kykkos they travelled to where the fighting was taking place in the north.

My brother-in-law Tasos, the husband of Chrystalla, has told me of the following story which my father doesn't speak about now. There are some things that he has chosen to put out of his mind.

From Kykkos my father went to an infantry unit in the vicinity of Morphou. The officer in charge of the unit had abandoned his post but my father took charge and told the soldiers what to do. He put them into trucks and without lights, and on track roads, drove them to a safe area near to Pyrgos. He saved the young soldiers lives.

They found the officer in the free areas and some of the soldiers wanted to kill him but my father stopped them. Because the soldiers had not met my father before they thought that he was a supporter of the Junta and were taken by surprise when they found out that he was in fact a socialist.

My sister Maro does remember one funny story though when a high-ranking officer gave orders to my father to go to meet some people in the mountains to collect dynamite. Kokos went with my father and the officer gave them a secret password *'we came to get the cypress tree'*.

They found a man at the spot where they had been told to go and gave him the password, whereupon the man insisted on giving them a load of cypress trees and sent them away. It must have been the wrong man!

My brother-in-law Tasos was himself due to join the army on the day of the invasion to do his national service but it was delayed. Twice during the period between the coup taking place, and the invasion of Cyprus, Tasos was beaten-up badly by supporters of EOKA-B, once when he was stopped at an unofficial road-block manned by EOKA-B in Limassol, and on the second occasion when he was chased near to an EOKA-B supporter's house.

***

At school we were doing drills for false alarms so everybody had to run in a line quickly out of the class into a ditch, one after the other with our heads down, and then we had to lie on the ground and keep very still.

For us children life was changing at a slow pace and I guess where we were living it was quite far from the war, and things were taking place gradually.

I was eight and a half years old at that time. I didn't really understand a lot. Just the *'fear in the ear'* but soon as children we were in our own world, playing at every opportunity we could get.

My father came to see us one night in the dark but he left almost immediately. His hand was wrapped in a bandage and he looked as if he was hurt."

***

The Greek military Junta collapsed on the 23 July 1974, mainly because of events in Cyprus, and was replaced by a democratic government.

In Cyprus Nikos Sampson renounced the presidency and Glafcos Clerides took over as the temporary President, just after midday, after being sworn in by the dethroned Bishop of Paphos.

Nikos Sampson made an address to the people and cited Clerides' experience as a negotiator as the reason for him standing down. It raised hopes in the community at large that Turkey might halt its military operation. They were to be proved wrong.

Peace talks involving the three 'guarantor' countries Turkey, Greece, and the United Kingdom, failed to make any progress in relation to resolving the escalating violence between the Greek and Turkish Cypriot communities.

During talks in Geneva on the 13 August the Turkish side put forward proposals for two territorial zones to be created, one for Turks, and the other for Greeks, on the basis of a federal arrangement. The total area under Turkish control would come to some 34% of the Island.

On that day a message was sent to the Turkish delegation, which included the Turkish Foreign Minister Turan Gunes. It read *'Turan Gunes's daughter visited me. I told her she can travel. Tell that to Turan Gunes.'* These in fact were the code words to signal that military preparations for the next part of the Turkish invasion were complete.

Between the 14th and 16th August 1974 a second Turkish invasion led to more than 37% of the island being captured and occupied, as part of *'Operation Attilla Two'*.

During this operation the Turkish regular army also deployed Turkish Cypriot members of *'TMT'* and there were widespread allegations that some of these forces were involved in looting and summary executions.

The operation began at 4.55am on 14 August, just one and a half hours after the collapse of the talks in Geneva, as the Turkish Air Force flew unheeded over Cyprus and hit targets for the next four hours.

The town of Famagusta fell to the Turks on the 14 August as advance Turkish soldiers entered the Turkish enclave at 5.30pm and then found that the area occupied by Greek Cypriots had been emptied of its inhabitants. To this day it is still referred to as a *'ghost town'* with parts of Famagusta classified as a restricted militarised area.

***

(Andry):

"When the invasion happened my grandfather Christos was a night-guard at a quarry somewhere near Kythrea. Turkish soldiers turned up at the quarry and were about to shoot him. He started asking them to spare his life and spoke to them in Turkish. A high-ranking officer heard him speak and ordered the soldiers to let him go. Somehow he also managed to hide his money by burying it but I don't know if he was able to recover it.

Two of my cousins, Koulis and Christakis, suffered a terrible experience during the invasion when, as teenagers, they were taken prisoner and transported to a prison camp in Adana in southern Turkey where they were held for nearly six months. Eventually their family were able to give their details to the International Red Cross and they found them and they were returned to Cyprus. Not everyone was fortunate enough to get home though and even today there are many people still missing.

My friend Koulla Mylona has her own memories of these days. She lived in a village called Skylloura, which is just a ten-minute drive to Nicosia. It was a mixed village with two thirds

Greek Cypriots and a third Turkish Cypriots. Although they generally got on they lived in separate areas in the village. Not far from them was a Turkish Cypriot village and they had previously caused problems for them during the troubles in the 1960s when a number of Greek Cypriots were killed after a Turkish Cypriot girl got pregnant after an affair with a Greek Cypriot.

Koulla was thirteen years old when the invasions happened and as Turkish troops got closer to her village her parents sent her away with her sister, while they stayed and gave food to the Greek Cypriot soldiers.

There was a Greek officer there from the National Guard and finally as the Turks entered the village from one end they all left in a car with a trailer attached to it from the other end and just managed to avoid some tanks.

It was two weeks before Koulla was able to be reunited with her parents again."

***

Ultimately a ceasefire line was established which became known as the United Nations Buffer Zone, and which is commonly referred to as the *'Green Line'*. It is a place where time has stood completely still as properties have been left to decay in the condition in which they were in when Cypriots, both Greek and Turkish, left in fear for their lives.

Finally 36.3% of Cyprus came under Turkish control, with The Republic of Cyprus retaining control of 60%, whilst 3.7% became a demilitarised zone.

After this invasion forty thousand Turkish troops were stationed in northern Cyprus, where two hundred and two towns and villages were affected by the movement of people.

Much of the area also had some of the most fertile farmland on the island.

At the time 80% of the northern occupied-area of the island was made up of Greek Cypriots, many of them farmers. Most of them were ultimately forcibly expelled to the south, whilst in due course up to 60,000 Turkish Cypriots were displaced to the north.

The total number of Greek Cypriot refugees from the conflict was initially estimated at between 140,000 to 160,000 people, giving a total of more than 200,000 displaced persons.

In those early days many people, from both communities, found themselves living in tents with nothing more than the few personal possessions that they had been able to carry.

***

Malcolm Halliday concludes his recollections of the time,

"At some stage an agreement was reached whereby Turkish Cypriot refugees would be flown from RAF Akrotiri in Turkish civilian planes to the Turkish mainland.

A demonstration was held by Greek Cypriots at the gates of RAF Akrotiri, protesting against these moves and the RAF Regiment struggled to control the demonstration, which turned violent. Vehicles and trucks were overturned and burnt, and bricks were thrown. My Battalion was picked up by RAF helicopters and flown inside.

We had experience of riots in Northern Ireland and were immediately deployed with pickaxe handles, rubber bullets and CS-Gas to disperse the crowds. We were backed up by scout-cars and dispersed the people back down the main road.

I left Cyprus about six months later – what should have been a *'rest and recuperation'* posting in the sun turned out to be far from it."

***

Before the Turkish invasion 180,000 Greek Cypriots and 44,000 Turkish Cypriots lived in the part of Cyprus that was under occupation, with up to 160,000 Greek Cypriots moving south. Another 71,000 Turkish Cypriots lived in the southern part of the island the majority of whom moved north.

Initially 20,000 Greek Cypriots remained enclaved in the Karpasia region on the easternmost tip of the Island, however less than a year later most of them were forcibly removed to the south. At the same time 60,000 Turkish settlers were brought from the Turkish mainland and settled in the occupied areas.

About three thousand people lost their lives during the conflict and many Greek Cypriots were taken to Turkey as prisoners of war.

***

There were some exceptions as people voluntarily moved, or were forced to move, north and south.

Hassan Moustafa, a Turkish Cypriot from Androlykou, in the centre of the Paphos district, fell in love with Hambou Pournoxouzi, a Greek Cypriot from the neighbouring village of Droushia in the late 1950s. Overcoming convention, family concerns, and religion they were the first mixed-couple to be married in the newly independent Republic of Cyprus, although at the time the law did not provide for an Orthodox Christian to marry a Muslim.

Their story was made into a Cyprus-made *'Romeo and Juliet'* film that was screened at the Venice Film Festival in 2006.

In 1975 over six hundred Turkish villagers left his village for the north under the terms of the post-war population exchange. Hassan and Hambou opted however to stay in Androlykou, hopeful that the Cyprus problem would be solved. He died in 2014 after having lived in the village for the whole of his life.

Today, in 2017, six Turkish Cypriot families, with mixed marriages, live in the village, and one of Hassan's four children Ezgur Hassan Moustafa, is the only Turkish Cypriot *'mukhtar'*, community leader, in the government controlled areas.

The village gives hope to the aspiration that Greek and Turkish Cypriots might once again co-exist in peace and harmony.

Androlykou is a village in the Akamas region, not far from the Evretou dam, where the local people own more than 3,000 goats and are mainly involved in farming.

***

During the course of these conflicts allegations of atrocities and human rights abuses were made by both sides. In some cases neighbours fought neighbours in communities where previously Greek and Turkish Cypriots had lived side-by-side.

Hundreds of people from both sides died during the fighting and hundreds of people were officially listed as missing. Most of these were soldiers or reservists, but the figures did include civilians, including women and young people.

A *'Committee of Missing Persons'* set up under the auspices of the United Nations gathered details of 992 soldiers/reservists reported as missing, together with 511 male civilians, and 116 female civilians – a total of 1,619 persons in all.

Many still remain missing to this day.

***

(Andry):

"When my father eventually returned home after a number of weeks he went into the Coffee Shop which all the EOKA-B supporters used. He had with him his gun, which he had a legal written permission to possess, and confronted them all demanding to know who was looking for him and that anyone had anything to say now was the time to speak.

None of them spoke and he walked out – he was a very brave man.

***

At some point the first refugee family came to live in Trachoni and soon afterwards more followed.

This led to the improvement of the village as the roads were fixed, new houses started to appear, and new people from different locations found a home there.

My school-friend Andry Ioannou remembers that after the invasion lots of tents were set up in the area of Ypsonas for Greek Cypriot refugees to live in temporarily. At Christmas her family took presents to give to some of the children that were living there in difficult conditions.

***

When the children caught fleas the boys at school used to have their heads shaved to get rid of them. There was a small corridor behind a building in the schoolyard where the boys used to hide and when their heads were like this the girls used to run through and slide their hands over their bald heads to tease them.

For the girls if we caught fleas we used to have our hair washed in vinegar and then the fleas were brushed out with a special brush.

I was aged nine by now and remember at this time that there was a man in the village, called Demetros, who was cleaning and looking after the church of Agios Mamas. I'm not sure if he was paid but he was always next to the priest Papas Skouloukos – Evaggelos.

Demetros had no hair at all on his face or head and people were calling him 'spanos, which was the description for a person who had no hair on his body, and he was also unable to have children. He was married with Milou.

They were very poor people - Demetros was a bit of a strong build, and had a big red face, whereas Milou was very thin.

Because they didn't have their own children they were always very kind to others.

I remember that after the invasion a big tent with armed British soldiers were camping on top of the hill that we call

Vounaros. Demetros was gathering together as many children as he could and we would all walk up there.

He used to introduce himself and with very little English was pointing to us saying that we were all his children. The soldiers would then go into the tent and would come out with a big cardboard box with lots of tins and anything that was edible. They would hold the box and we were all jumping to pick anything from inside to eat. It could be cheese, in like a toothpaste container, chocolates, or sweets.

Anything was welcome and we would then run away like goats down the hill, happy and satisfied as we went back home. I wasn't speaking any English at that time as at school we were only starting English lessons at the age of eleven, the last year of elementary school.

I don't think the soldiers ever realised that it wasn't always the same group of children that Demetros used to bring to visit them!

Eventually as well as the big new school being built, there was a bigger church, and more mini-markets for food shopping were opened.

Before the new elementary school on the hill next to the church was finished a campaign took place in order to make the area around the school green and beautiful. Lots of pine trees and others were planted by the students and teachers."

Figure 42 Rock of Aphrodite – Paphos – Michalis/Maro

(circa 1974)

Figure 43 Rock of Aphrodite – Paphos – Roulla (circa

1974)

Figure 44 Trachoni – Michalis/Andry on pedal

cycle/Chrystalla/Despo/Roulla (circa 1974)

Figure 45 Limassol Old Port – Andry's father

Costas/Michalis/Andry's mother Loukia (circa 1974)

235

Figure 46 Andry's father Costas as a volunteer soldier (circa 1974)

Figure 47 Andry's father Costas as a volunteer soldier with a Greek officer (circa 1974)

Figure 48 Picture of the certificate for bravery awarded to

Andry's father for his actions in 1974

Figure 49 Tasos Charalambous – 1974

Figure 50 Chrystalla/Roulla/Despo/Loukia –

mother/Michalis/Maro/Andry seated (circa 1974)

Figure 51 Wedding of Kokos and Maro (5 May 1974) – Andry

sat in front

Figure 52 3rd Grade Elementary School Trachoni Class Photo –

Andry far left middle row – 1973/1974

Figure 53 A roadblock at Avdimou – Malcolm Halliday on far

right (July 1974) (Ack - MH)

Figure 54 The aftermath of a demonstration at RAF Akrotiri –

(1974) (Ack - MH)

Figure 55 David Woolmer RAF (circa 1974) in Cyprus (Ack -

DW)

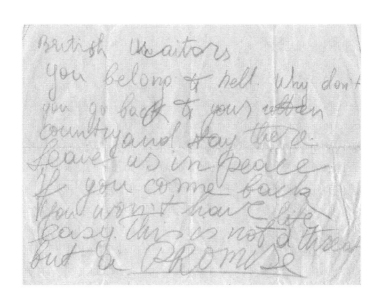

Figure 56 An original note left at David Woolmer's address in

Platres, Cyprus following the invasion in 1974 (Ack - DW)

Chapter Eleven

1975

Food & More Food

On the 13 February 1975, Turkey declared the *'occupied areas'* of the Republic of Cyprus to be a *'Federated Turkish State'*, in a move that was condemned by the United Nations, and the international community. Some years later it became known as the *'Turkish Republic of Northern Cyprus'* (TRNC). The only country to recognise it is Turkey.

In the same year civilian settlers began arriving from the mainland in Turkey to settle in northern Cyprus. Estimates put their numbers at 120,000.

***

(Andry):

"As a poor family we couldn't afford to buy land in order to build a house. Someone said to my father that if we moved to

Trachoni and rented for a year then we would be entitled to get a piece of land and build. They were trying to encourage people to live there because the population was so small.

So that's the reason we moved to Trachoni. A year after we moved there we chose a piece of land that we thought was okay to build on and made a start.

My father though was very tight with the money and wouldn't buy anything new. As I recall all of the windows and doors for the house were second-hand from other buildings.

We moved in just before Michalis was born and it is still our family home today where my mother lives.

At some stage after the invasion my grandparents Irinou and Christos came to stay with us for a while in Trachoni. My grandmother was a big lady with blue eyes and my grandfather was a bit short with a big white moustache.

My grandmother was in her late-seventies then and one day she said that she wanted to go to the little chapel, Ayios Georgios, near our house, to light a candle. My mother asked me to go with her to keep her company and off we went.

It was about a ten-minute walk and as we reached the place my grandmother needed urgently to go to the toilet for a *'poo'* and she walked behind a rock and sat there for a while.

Suddenly she started shouting for me to wipe her bottom. As I went close she gave me a piece of paper – I wasn't happy at all and was disgusted but I had no option. She was a big lady and simply couldn't reach her bottom to clean herself!

I told my mother what happened when I got back and everyone started laughing at me. At home my mother was used to washing her to keep her clean and was used to it.

It was ironic that despite Irinou not going to her wedding she was quite happy in the end for my mother to look after her!

Irinou could be quite difficult at times and I remember one day she had an argument with Roulla as a result of which she pushed her outside and then locked the door behind her.

Irinou always used to call me *'Andriani'* instead of Androulla. I didn't like it but again I had no choice.

Because my grandparents were refugees they were given some help every week with rice, sugar and some tins of pork and corned beef. I used to go with my grandfather to help him to pick it up and he would always buy me an ice cream as a treat.

We also used to go together to pick figs from the trees near to the chapel. The fig tree belonged to the Turkish Cypriot that used to live there. I jumped to catch a fig one day and pulled a leaf which went into my eye. This is very dangerous because the leaves have spikes on them and they have like sticky milk inside which can damage your eye. Fortunately my grandfather managed to get it out for me!

When my grandfather first moved into our house he amazed us when he picked up all our plant-pots with flowers in, took them across the road, and dumped them in a ditch which was full of rubbish.

He said that flowers didn't produce food so there was no reason to have them.

We had some beautiful flowers and we tried to recover what we could. He even threw a large cactus plant away which we had grown for some time into a very large plant. It had flowers on it that closed in the day and opened at night.

On another occasion my grandmother asked my mother to cook her some specific food.

My mother did as she asked but when it was ready she went into the kitchen, had a look under the lids of the cooking pots, then turned and went back to her rooms, at the back of the house.

When my father came home my grandmother complained that she had been left to go hungry.

My mother was at her wits end with the situation and lost a lot of weight because of the stress. She went as thin as a stick and finally told my father that she couldn't take any more – my grandparents would need to find somewhere else to stay.

At some point they lived in a house which had previously been lived in by Turkish Cypriots in Kofinou, which is situated between Larnaca and Limassol, and we used to visit them.

My grandmother still liked a lot of attention and I used to regularly comb her hair. She had two plats normally and she would sit outside in the sun whilst I undid them, combed her white long hair, and then put them back into plats again, before rolling them around her head.

Some years later, because they felt that they were too far away from the rest of the family, they finally got a grant from the government and built two rooms on the land that was given to me by the Trachoni Council to build my home in the future. This is where they lived then until they died.

This didn't cause me any problems and in the end it was my grandfather who was literally doing everything for my grandmother, washing and feeding her. She spent her last years just sat in a chair during the day."

***

In April 1975 fighting broke out between Maronite and Palestinian forces in the Lebanon and a civil war ensued. During the 1960s some 400,000 Palestinian refugees settled there and the Palestinian

Liberation Organisation gained a major foothold with the creation of a *'State within a State'.*

The conflict led to Arab and Muslim groups forming an alliance with the PLO as it fought with Christian groupings.

The proximity of Lebanon to Cyprus made it an attractive option for some to escape the war.

***

(Andry):

"At some point I became very close to Mary who was our neighbour. She was the elder child of three at this time but the only girl. She was playing the guitar and I was singing at school solo, or with the choir.

Mary was very beautiful and I used to admire her. She was a couple of years older than me but this didn't stop us being friends. Her mother Troodia was a friend of my mother's too. In years to come we lost touch but I know that she would always stand next to me. Now she is married with two grown-up children.

We used to collect green olives and put them into a bucket of water, high on the trees or on the roof of her house, pretending to make them into *'tsakkistes'*. This is a dish with olives, made with lemon, olive oil, garlic and coriander, with smashed-up olives in salt water. Whatever was going wrong with ours though they finished up with worms!

Around Mary's house they had a lot of land planted with pears, lemon trees, oranges and mandarins. As a child I used to help during the time that the fruits were picked. Because I was so small and light I could climb trees like a monkey and get to the highest point of a tree to get those furthest away. I also got the chance to eat some of the largest and juiciest ones!

After some years, when the export of some of these fruits became difficult, the oranges and pear trees were replaced with olive trees.

Olive trees have been grown in Cyprus for more than four thousand years, and there is a tree near the village of Ayia Marina, which is said to be more than seven hundred years old.

When the British ran the country they increased the production of olives and now there are believed to be more than two million trees growing on the island.

We planted about five olive trees at our house after it was built and after a couple of years they started to provide olives - *'elies'*. They can be harvested at any point from green when they are immature to when they are fully ripened. How they are harvested depends on what the olives are going to be used for.

If they are for eating they have to be handpicked to avoid bruising. If they are for oil production they can be harvested by putting tarpaulins on the ground around the tree, then raking each branch so that they fall onto them to be gathered up.

The whole family would get involved as the work has to be done quickly and wet weather has to be avoided as the olives can be spoilt. Any that fall onto the ground have to be picked up otherwise there is a risk that they will rot and cause diseases.

The earlier you harvest olives the more bitter they will taste, and they are preserved in brine. Normally we would do it about October/November time.

Green olives picked when they are full size, but before they are ripened, usually progress to shades of yellow.

Those which are semi-ripe go from green to shades of red to brown.

Those which are ripe at full maturity go from brown to black. Olive oil has long been considered sacred, and is one of the three blessed products, wine, wheat and olive oil. During a baptism olive oil is used to cross the child and the leaves from olive trees are used as incense in churches.

In the bible the dove that brought Noah an olive branch from God was a sign that he was extending mercy and the floods stopped.

The olive branch is also a symbol of abundance, glory and peace, purity and fertility. The leafy branches of the olive tree were used to make crowns for the victors in battles and at organised games.

About every ten years you have to prune the trees right back to the main branches which will then grow again within three years.

We still have our olive trees growing in the back garden of our house to this day and every year we gather the olives and take them to a factory to have the oil extracted.

***

We had one black and white TV in the house and I remember that my favourite programmes were *'Skippy the Kangaroo', 'Flipper the Dolphin', 'Star Ship Enterprise'* and *'The Little House on the Prairie'* with my favourite character Laura who had a younger sister Carrie.

They lived in a house in Walnut Grove, in America and at school a girl called Nellie Oleson was always causing problems. We used to sit on the sofa at home waiting for these programmes to come on and if they changed the schedules we would get very upset!

***

One of the most famous actors that we used to love watching in films on the TV was Aliki Vougiouklaki. She was born in Greece in 1934 and was very beautiful.

She was best known for films and theatrical plays, as well being a theatrical producer and was given the title, *'The National Star of Greece'* as she created renditions of well-known Broadway hits and Greek tragedy plays.

Her last movie was *'Kataskopos Nelly' (Nelly The Spy)* in 1981 and for ten years she was married to Dimitris Pamamichael who was an actor and fellow theatre student. He was very handsome.

I remember one of her films was called *'Ena Asteio Koritsi' (A Funny Girl)* in which she actually played a happy character. She was dressed as a clown to make people happy but she was actually very unhappy in her personal life. This was just for the film.

When she first started acting she had brown hair, and then later became blonde. One of her trademarks was to wear a red Hibiscus flower behind her ear.

Aliki died from pancreatic cancer in 1996, aged sixty-two years, but they showed pictures of her at her funeral and you would have said that she was in her twenties. Her wish was to die young and for people to remember her as young and beautiful.

***

We liked seeing the animals on the programmes and my father used to take us as a family quite often to the zoo in Limassol, which was within the Municipal Park, near the seafront.

Within the park there were lots of areas where goldfish used to swim amongst the plants in concrete channels about twelve inches deep but they are all dry now.

There were two elephants in the zoo called *'Adam'* and *'Julie'* and on one occasion my father was teasing one of them by holding out his closed hand and pretending to have nuts in it. Each time the elephant put his trunk out to take something he showed him the empty palm of his hand and was laughing.

After doing this a couple of times the elephant got upset and suddenly spat a load of gooey stuff out of his trunk which hit my father's chest. The good thing was that it missed his face but we all thought it was hilarious!

Sometime later one of these elephants killed one of his keepers by stamping on his head.

There were also a couple of bears in a cage there plus a lion and a lioness. The space that they kept them in was not ideal for keeping animals and eventually they were given away to other zoos.

***

From since before I can remember I was an *'Omonia Football Club'* supporter.

My father was a big Omonia fan and used to get very emotional when he went to the games. Eventually when he developed a heart condition he had to stop going because the excitement was too much for him.

All of my family are Omonia fans, and generally support political parties on the left, such as SK-EDEK. They say that there are so many Omonia fans they are called *'The Chinese'.*" as the Chinese are millions!"

***

OMONIA FC - Athletic Club Omonia of Nicosia, which means *'Concord'* in Greek, was set up on the 4 June 1948. The team colours are green and white team and for years they have been seen as the team of the Cyprus *'working class'*.

The club are seen as being to the left of politics in Cyprus and influenced by political unrest and the Greek civil war. Many support the AKEL party.

They play at the GSP Stadium in Nicosia. The club is the one of the *'Big Five'* teams in Cyprus and they have won league championships, Cypriot Cup competitions, and Super Cups.

The club also acts as an umbrella for other sports and fields teams in basketball, volleyball, cycling, and futsal.

One poll by the University of Cyprus once ranked Omonia as the second most popular team behind APOEL, whilst in yet another poll 26.8% of those polled said that they supported Omonia.

By the end of February 2013 Omonia was struggling to meet UEFA's financial conditions, due in part to the economic downturn. In March 2013 however they managed to pass the criteria due to a fundraising initiative which was launched under the slogan *'I'm with Omonia. I declare present'*.

More than 3.5 million euro was raised in less than a month.

***

(Andry):

"If we got sick at all my mother used to rub *'Zivania'* on our backs. It is a spirit with a high alcohol content and is distilled from grapes.

When drunk by adults it is usually served very cold from the freezer, but many Cypriots believe strongly in its medicinal benefits for the digestive system, headaches and colds.

There is another treatment called *'kazzi'* or *'ventouza'* using *'Zivania'*. The *'Zivania'* would be heated up to burn the oxygen and put onto a spoon which had been wrapped with cotton round it. It was then put into the *'ventouza'* and very quickly placed on your back whilst hot. It would make dark marks wherever it was placed as the *'ventouza'* was sucking the skin in."

***

The ancient art of 'cupping' is a method of causing local congestion, where a vacuum is created with the use of vessels, which are placed on the skin either by means of heat or suction, which then draws up the underlying tissues.

When the cups, anything up to five, are left in place for a few minutes localised healing takes place as the flow of blood and toxins are stimulated and muscles massaged.

*****

Food continues to occupy the hearts and minds of Cypriots to this day and is very much a part of the solder that welds family life together:

(Andry):

"We use a phrase *'love starts from the stomach'* and believe that if you cook well people will love you because of it.

Very traditional is the *'karidaki'* sweet which is the walnut before it becomes hard. So when it is soft on the tree they collect it and peel the outside slightly. Then they put it in water for eight to ten days, together with a small quantity of asbestos, to take all the bitterness away. It was only later that they discovered that this was poisonous.

Then they put it in syrup and for three days boil it for a little time each day. Finally it's ready to be eaten - crunchy and soft at the same time, black like velvet but very delicious. The syrup is considered to be good for coughs.

My mother used to make them every year, and during the month of April her hands would be coloured black from peeling the walnuts.

One type of food that was always welcome, and one that we had regularly, when the season was right, were stuffed marrow flowers. Up until today it is still done by my mother in the most delicious way. The ingredients are all fresh so in the morning with the first touch of the sunlight my mother would be out in the back garden, collecting the marrow flowers, before the heat of the day took hold. This is important because the flowers close after a couple of hours and so are not able to be stuffed.

The next step is to cut the little green stems out from the flower, to wash them thoroughly and then to put them to dry.

Then all of the ingredients are put into a big pot, normally rice, small freshly-cut onions, lots of parsley, dry mint, cinnamon and black pepper, salt, lots of fresh tomatoes, juice blended at the time, and small cuts of carrots, marrow or even mushrooms, and some olive oil.

After this the marrow flowers are stuffed and the tops closed carefully by bending the flower inside.

They are then placed in a circle in a cooking pot. A couple of chicken stocks are melted in a hot glass of water and poured on the top with some lemon.

They are then cooked for thirty to forty minutes.

Everybody was happy with this meal and at the side with it would be a thick village yogurt.

***

On the 7 September 1975 my sister Maro had her first child Kostas. There were no arguments about what to name him as both grandparents were called Kostas! He is the first grandchild in our family.

At some point I made my own vegetable garden at the side of our home. I was really very proud of it as I did it all by myself and really enjoyed it.

At the time I had a three-wheeled bicycle. Most probably somebody gave it to my father as I don't remember him buying it. But I was very happy to ride it up and down the street which was more like a track road.

Further down from our house was an empty field that at the time belonged to nobody. It used to be owned by some Turkish Cypriots that left after the Turkish invasion. So with a bucket to each side of my bike I took the red soil from that field and filled up a corner of our garden on the left hand side of our home.

The whole garden was empty, as we had no money to bring lots of soil to fill it up and plant anything there. The area was rocky and nothing grew unless additional soil was placed on top.

I had to go up and down several times and I got very tired but I didn't give up.

I also fertilised the soil with *'natural'* vitamins from sheep, and goat poo that I also picked up from around the area, as some families had sheepfolds. A good mixture with the soil was the perfect combination for my vegetables.

Almost opposite our house was the sheepfold of Kirios Efremis and Kiria Panayiota.

Efremis was a slim tall man and Panayiota was short and quite big. They were the grandparents of a schoolmate Panayiota who I grew up with throughout my younger years.

Kiria Panayiota was making the most delicious and thick Greek yogurt, which we were buying, and it was always on the kitchen table for our meals. They also made very special haloumi and we could never get enough of it.

As the sheepfold was so close it was also easy to collect the *'vitamins'* for my growing vegetables.

I filled up my corner and next step I planted it with aubergines, peppers, green and spicy, lettuce and tomatoes.

I was so proud of my little vegetable garden and soon my aubergines grew so high that I could bend them and crawl underneath. Every day I would check to see what was ready to eat.

I liked what I did so I brought some more soil and made another corner for some chrysanthemums. By October all the flowers had bloomed in lots of colour, yellow, purple and pink. Sometimes I took a bunch of them to school for the school vase. Whenever there was an opportunity we tried to make our classroom beautiful with some fresh flowers from our gardens, or some wild lily's that used to grow up the hill.

I wasn't picking only wild lilies from the hill. During winter and just after any rain, snails were coming out. For us in Cyprus they are considered to be a delicacy and part of our *'meze'* so as I was going to school in the morning I was collecting, in a plastic nylon bag, snails that came out of the wet ground.

Sometimes I had to look for them in the bushes and would scratch my hands from the nettles. But sometimes they were out moving or trying to mate so there would be like five or six stuck together.

Most of the time we would put them in a bucket to clean up for a day or two and feed them with some flour or oats before washing them a couple of times.

Then we would boil them until they came out of their shells with no effort using a toothpick. Finally we dipped them in a bowl of half vinegar and half olive oil before eating them.

Another way to cook them was with rice. First we boiled the snails and cut the highest point of the shell mixing them with rice before cooking. Sometimes we put them on a plate after boiling and put salt and olive oil with crushed garlic over them and then cooked them in the oven for a while before eating.

There are different kinds of snails. The green ones are not for eating as we say that they live in cemeteries. Big brown snails are good, as well as white ones with brown stripes, and some kind of a mini snail that gather on wild bushes, and are served in tavernas.

My life as a child was very simple. We were very poor but we somehow managed. My mum always was making sure that we ate well and we had a warm bed and clean clothes. We had almost all kinds of domestic animals in the back garden; chickens for eggs, which were fresh and red in colour.

We had big rabbits and Guinea pigs for meat, pigeons for eating, ducks, turkeys, and a goat for the fresh milk every morning.

I remember we always had a *'fight'* over who was going to get the top of the milk after it was boiled. That was like a skin and was very thick and tasty.

At some point we had a beautiful tree which produced large peaches that were so delicious and sweet. We had a couple of fig trees at both sides of the house, and at the front to the right a *'mespilia'* tree.

The fruit from this tree was about the size of a plum when ripe and the colour of apricots. The taste is a little like the combined taste of an apricot and plum, although there are three or four large stones in each fruit. Sometimes the birds used to eat them before us.

Covering the whole of the front garden was a flower called *'Afros tis Afroditis'*. The name means *'Foam of Afrodity'* and the leaves were half white and half green. It looked like snow. Initially I had just one small plant from my friend Olga's garden, and then it just spread and took over the whole garden.

Once a week I also remember that a man used to come to the village on a pedal cycle to sell *'pastelaki'* from two big baskets which he had either side of the bike. This is a thick brown product, which is chewy and comes from the carob tree. It tastes a bit like marmite.

We used to save empty pots of shoe-colour or any other glass bottles to give to him in exchange for a piece of the *'pastelaki'*.

***

I remember once when I was at the fourth grade at the elementary school and my younger sister Despo was in the second grade, one of her schoolmates made her cry. I don't remember exactly what happened but she came to me crying saying that Elena had hit her.

Elena was a big girl and my sister was really tiny.

Elena's brother Mimis (Dimitris was the full name) was in my class so to get revenge on Elena I confronted Mimis. I stood in front of him and I said, "Your sister punched my sister so I will punch you to get equal." I then started kicking him and pulling his hair. He was a big boy but this didn't stop me.

As the school year was not very big everybody saw us fighting, even the teacher Mr Antonis Papadopoulos. He found it a bit amusing as I was managing with a big boy but eventually he separated us and told us to calm down and to behave ourselves. Mimis was not an aggressive boy after all whereas I was a bit feisty!

Our school consisted of just two big classrooms but it was enough when I started there. At some point after the invasion some refugee families came to live in the village so the school rented a room from the nearby house which we were using as an extra classroom. Another room was just a couple of minutes further so every time we had a break we had to queue in a line in pairs and walk to the schoolyard.

Mr Papadopoulos was a very good teacher. He was trying hard for us to teach us and to make progress. He always gave a prize which was a book for every time we improved in handwriting, spelling or reading. I remember that I had the prize for handwriting improvement once, and for my efforts I was given a Jules Verne book.

I liked the books of Jules Verne so I read quite a few like *'Captain Nemo'*, and *'Around the World in Eighty Days'*.

I was very competitive at that age and I never liked to come second!

But there were quite a few of us girls that were good students – Liso, Olga, Pantelitsa, Argyroulla, Giota to name just a few.

One thing that I was really good at as well was acting and singing. Many times I got the main role and some of the other girls didn't like it, especially those that were older than me. But Mr Papadopoulos was always giving us the role to read out loud and the best one was getting it.

I played the child that visited the new born Jesus at the Christmas show at the school.

I remember being dressed in long nightwear and I was feeling embarrassed to walk on the stage with my nightwear but I did it and the play was very successful.

When I was about ten a stray dog turned up at our house. He was gold-coloured like a collie, and as children we adopted him. He was living outside but he started to kill the neighbour's rabbits and chickens and my mother didn't want him.

Despo was very close to the dog which we named *'Lucky'*. It used to follow her to school and then go back later to walk back with her when she finished. Sometimes it would hold her bag in its mouth as they walked.

The dog had an ear infection and one day he just disappeared - but we have a feeling that finally he wasn't so lucky and that my parents had taken him away in the car and left him somewhere."

Figure 57 Nr. Nicosia – Andry's grandfather Christos 'Mavris'

& Andry's mother Loukia (circa 1975)

Figure 58 Nr. Nicosia – Andry's grandfather Christos 'Mavris'

& Andry's father Costas (circa 1975)

Figure 59 Nr. Nicosia – Family gathering – Andry front row (circa 1975)

Figure 60 Agios Athanasios – Andry (circa 1975)

Figure 61 Trachoni – Andry's father Costas with his new car

(circa 1975)

Figure 62 Trachoni – 4th grade Elementary Class – Andry

middle row far left (12.4.1975)

Chapter Twelve

1976

Another Marriage

(Andry):

"I had one of my first boyfriends during this period – his name was Alekos Constantinou and he lived in the village. His father was called Panicos Constantinou who had been involved with the Cooperative Bank in the village. Even as young children we had to have a boyfriend or girlfriend and he was the one I chose. There was no kissing or holding hands though – just good friendship.

Alekos still lives in the village of Trachoni to this day and has his own construction business.

When we gave the kiosk up my father used to take us all in the summer in his car early to the same spot on a beach by the New Port. It's not there anymore because the port has been extended to take containers. We used to swim all day and sit under an umbrella whilst my father was working at the port as a Customs officer.

My father used to wear a white uniform and this has always remained his favourite colour for clothing.

At lunchtime he would come and see us and then go back to work before picking us up in the evening to go home. We were all there with my mother except for Maro."

***

"Sami became a friend of my father's because he had his yacht in the port at Limassol where my father worked. He was a Palestinian living in Lebanon but like a lot of others he moved to Cyprus as a result of the fighting there.

He studied in Europe and had been a captain on ships. His yacht wasn't that big but it had a cabin that you could sit and eat in and he used it to travel between Lebanon and Cyprus.

My father brought Sami home a couple of times to eat and it seemed that Sami liked Roulla, and she liked him, so he asked if he could marry her.

They got engaged on Roulla's eighteenth birthday.

He was a Muslim and they had a civil ceremony in Limassol, the following year, but my father's family insisted that they should also have a church wedding. Sami agreed to be baptised in the Christian Orthodox faith so that he could take a certificate to say he was a Christian, and took private lessons in order to know what to do.

The family went to Ayios Mamas Church in Trachoni and Sami stood in a big bath wearing his shorts whilst the holy water and oil was poured all over him. His godfather was *'Kokkinos'* who was in the same political party as my father, and a friend. I remember that we were all very discreet and just wanted to keep the service to family. We stood there trying not to laugh as Sami stood there soaking wet.

Sami's family rejected him initially after the ceremony because he had renounced his religion.

Eventually Sami's younger brother Mohamed came to visit from Lebanon, and his sister Alia, as well as his mother Suraya. She taught us how to do a traditional waxing technique called

'*Chalaoua*' which involves mixing sugar and water together with a few drops of lemon.

It becomes like a caramel substance which you apply to the skin. It weakens the hair from the root, sticks to the hair and not the skin, and so is less painful. It leaves you with very nice skin.

Sami and Roulla eventually got married in church in Trachoni and friends and family from our side attended.

They stayed with my mother for a while and did build above my parents' house but at one point they also rented a flat in Yermasogia, the tourist area in Limassol. My mother was very strict and even when Roulla was married she once shouted for her to come home as she was late after she had gone to a friend's house for a coffee.

Michalis remembers another couple of mishaps that he was involved in.

As Sami and Roulla started to build above my mother's we all tried to help with any way that we could, like carrying the brick blocks to the roof, and make coffees and sandwiches for the workers.

On this occasion Michalis remembers that he decided to explore the new building on his own. So as he was next to us and our mother he walked into one of the other rooms and onto the balcony. The whole place was a building site with concrete, bricks and tools everywhere. It was certainly not a place for a child.

As he was on the balcony he lost his balance and fell from it to the first floor. Somehow he bounced off the wires that my grandfather had placed for my mother to hang the washing out and from there was bounced onto the balcony of our kitchen. Luckily he didn't fall to the ground which was full of rocks and hard stones.

He ended up in hospital with a fracture to his cheek and a broken arm. The incident scared us all to death and afterwards we were very careful with him.

On another occasion Michalis was playing with Kyriakos at his house. Close by were some beehives which the father of Kyriakos kept bees in for making honey.

They decided to go and explore the boxes and the next thing that happened was that the bees started to attack them. Both of the boys started running and screaming as they were stung by the bees.

Michalis had hair which was a bit long and curly and all the bees were trapped in it.

Kyriakos finished up in hospital as he was allergic to the stings and his body started to swell up. He was in real danger!

Michalis was not so bad but to get rid of the bees my mother decided to spray his head with an aerosol which she used to spray for the flies.

It was an adventure that no-one forgot.

***

At some point Sami opened a restaurant in Limassol serving Lebanese food. It was called *'Shahrazad'*.

The name of the restaurant comes from the following Arabian tale.

'A King was shocked to find that his wife had been unfaithful to him so he had her executed. Believing that all women were the same he decided to marry a new woman each day who was a virgin, and then execute his new bride the following day so that it could never happen to him again. More than 1,000 women died in this

fashion until he met 'Scheherazade' who was an extremely well read
and educated woman.

Knowing what her likely fate was to be on her wedding night
she started to tell a story which the King listened to with great
interest. However she only half-finished the story so he spared her
for another day so that she could finish it.

Each night she finished a story and then half-started another
one. Day by day she managed to stay alive until she had told 1,000
stories after 1,001 nights by which time the King had fallen in love
with her and spared her life.'

The restaurant was very successful and they did well but
Sami had problems with his taxes. There were lots of rich Lebanese
in Cyprus at the time and many of them visited the restaurant where
you would often see opened bottles of champagne, costing up to fifty
Cyprus Pounds each, lined up around the dance-floor for the singers.
People would also throw flowers and money onto the stage.

On one of his trips from Lebanon, on one of the big ships, he
brought a German Shepherd puppy back called *'Rex'*. He was a
beautiful dog and very protective towards us all. One day when the

dog was at our house in Trachoni the brother of Mary, whose name was Kyriakos Athanatos, had a fight with my brother Michalis.

The name *'Athanatos'* means *'immortal'* in Greek.

They were actually close friends but whilst they were playing at the front of our house Kyriakos beat Michalis who started crying.

They were only children but *'Rex'* wasn't happy and started barking and chased Kyriakos back to his house, where he hid in the kitchen.

At this point, after making his point, *'Rex'* wandered back to comfort Michalis.

Whilst Sami was away on a trip the dog was staying with us. We took him to the beach at Ladies Mile and he was wandering around when the Health Department turned up on one of their patrols. There were some sheepfolds in the area and there had been reports of dogs attacking the sheep.

When the people from the Health Department saw *'Rex'* they thought that he was a stray dog and shot him. The dog cried out, dropped to the ground and died.

The people who had shot him started to drive away but my father chased them and stopped them. All they did was apologise and then left. It was very sad – we all really loved the dog and we cried for days for his loss. He was so much loved that we couldn't believe that he was gone.

On another of his trips to Lebanon in the yacht Sami was nearly killed after his yacht was blown up in one of the ports there. Two other people were killed and he was the only survivor. We all loved him very much because he gave us attention.

Whenever he went shopping he brought us lots of food and if he was cooking he used to cook one chicken each for every person!

He liked to watch international football on the TV and sometimes I would watch it with him. He used to drink tea from very small glasses, but whilst watching football it was a very large bottle of Carlsberg beer.

Sami and Roulla had two children during this period – a daughter Lina, two years after they were married, and a son also named Sami. Later in life they had another son named Daniel.

Roulla's husband Sami later died after the effects of regular drinking seriously affected his health, and during this period my sister saw another side to him.

She remembers that although he was a Palestinian he actually had a Jordanian passport and did not use his proper name for fear that the Israelis would find him as he had previously been involved in fighting there.

Sami obtained two Jordanian passports for Sami and Lina and every time they argued he would threaten to disappear with the children through the North. He was friends with the Jordanian ambassador in Cyprus and believed that he was capable of carrying out his threat.

Although the restaurant did well Roulla recalls that he also went into partnership with another man to set up an import/export company but the other man had lots of debts and all the money was going to help him.

Finally when the restaurant closed Sami's drinking got worse – he could easily drink a bottle of whisky a day and when Roulla finally banned him from the house he slept on the roof for a while in a small room that she used for the laundry. But this happened years later."

***

(Andry):

"During the fifth and sixth grades, at the elementary school, I trained in running and jumping over hurdles. I was the fastest out of all the girls and boys with the exception of Tryfonas.

They started giving us a *'sisitio'* at school which was a kind of breakfast which some of us welcomed and some not. It was a cup of hot milk and a toast of bread with some cheese or ham on top. The girls in the school were helping with the preparation during the school terms.

This *'sisitio'* cost me my involvement in a school athletic competition as once I was running to get my milk and toast and I fell on the ground and fractured my right knee. I ended up in hospital with a bandage on my knee for a month before I recovered.

I couldn't take part in the competition and that was it.

That year, before June 1976, it was taking place in Akrotiri village and the girl who came first was Soulla.

Soulla was one of the three girls who lost their lives on 13 March 1981 when the school bus she was in crashed and fell into a dam in the Troodos mountains.

***

We didn't have money for things like dentists in those days and when a tooth needed 'shaking out' we would take some cotton and tie it around the tooth before tying the other end to the knob on a door. We would then shut the door quickly and the tooth came out!

After this we would throw the old tooth onto the roof of the house and ask the *'fairies'* to bring us another strong one! We did though have mobile dentists who used to visit the schools and give us a free check-up.

***

It was normal for boys to play football at school but definitely not something for the girls to get involved in. In our last grades we girls decided to start playing football against the boys – we were actually quite good!

Nobody could take the ball away from me or they risked being kicked on the knees and we enjoyed it very much. Unfortunately the headmaster did not see it the same way.

One day he started shouting and said that it was bad enough having the boys stinking of sweat in the class after they had been playing football and now he had to put up with the girls stinking and covered in dust as well. That was it – we stopped."

***

On 20 December 1976, three monks, Abbot Stephanos aged eighty-two years, his seventy-seven year old brother Varnavas, and eighty-two year old Nektarios, who had lived at the Monastery of Saint Varnavas, near Famagusta, for sixty years, were evicted by Turkish Cypriot authorities.

The monastery was built in 477 AD at the spot where Saint Varnavas was buried.

***

(Andry):

"My sister Despo remembers that in 1976 the family had another experience with an owl when she found one sitting in the street as she walked home. The owl didn't move as she approached it and as she walked round it the owl just moved its head to follow her. It was a small owl, white and grey in colour, and made no sound whatsoever.

Despo decided to pick it up and take it home and strangely it didn't try to struggle or fly away at all. My mother got very angry with her for bringing another animal into the house, and she took it outside and threw it – she was worrying that we were going to have bad luck!"

Chapter Thirteen

1977

Death Of A President - *'The Happy One'* – *Makarios III*

Michail Christodoulou Mouskos was born in Panayia Village, Paphos, Cyprus on 13 August 1913. He was admitted, at the age of thirteen years, as a novice to Kykkos Monastery, and years later after completing his studies became a priest in the Greek Orthodox Church.

In 1948, whilst studying theology in America he was made the Bishop of Kition, against his will, at which point he adopted the clerical name Makarios.

Like many public figures in Cyprus in the 1940s and 1950s he was an active supporter of *'Enosis'*, the union of Cyprus with Greece.

On 18 September 1950, at the age of thirty-seven years, he was elected Archbishop of Cyprus.

On the 7 March 1953 Makarios, with ten other men, met at a house in Athens where they signed an oath confirming their full support for Enosis. They pledged that they were prepared to give their lives for the cause and would adhere to absolute secrecy. Colonel George Grivas signed the same oath a few days later.

After the collapse of talks with the British on the 9 March 1956 Makarios was arrested, together with three others, and deported without trial to the Seychelles in the Indian Ocean. They were to remain there for the next thirteen months.

Following a truce, which was declared by Grivas on the 14 March 1957, Makarios was released, on 6 April 1957, but was not allowed to return to Cyprus at that stage. Whilst remaining in Athens, dialogue continued with the British, both directly and indirectly.

In September 1958, during an interview with a British newspaper, Makarios acknowledged that he was now prepared to forego *'Enosis'* and to pursue independence instead.

Negotiations continued, but this change of direction did not go down well with Grivas.

Makarios returned to Cyprus on 1 March 1959 after the terms of agreement for independence were reached. He received a hero's welcome from thousands of people outside the Archbishop's Palace in Nicosia and announced to the crowd, *'NENIKHKAMEN – We have won!'*

Whilst he was praised by many for freeing Cyprus from the *'bondage of British colonialism'* others remained disappointed at his inability to bring about union with Greece.

It was an issue that would simply not go away.

Perhaps in a sign of things to come a separate rally was held in the Turkish part of Nicosia, which was addressed by Turkish Cypriot leader Dr. Fazil Kutchuk, who said, *'Although the Greeks may control the steering wheel of the state vehicle the Turkish Cypriots are in charge of the brakes.'*

On the 13 December 1959 Archbishop Makarios became the first President of the Republic of Cyprus.

During his three terms as President he survived four assassination attempts and the 1974 coup.

One of these attempts on his life occurred on the 8 March 1970, as he was about to fly in the Presidential helicopter to a memorial service for the deputy leader of EOKA, Gregoris Afxentiou. He had already been made aware that his life was in danger from elements with links to the Greek Military Junta in Cyprus, including the KYP intelligence services, but chose to continue with his daily duties.

The KYP Secret Service, otherwise known as the *'Central Information Service',* was founded by Makarios in 1970. Although an arm of the police working in plain-clothes, and undercover, many of them in the early years had *'trade-mark'* thick moustaches which pointed towards them being police officers.

As soon as the helicopter took off it came under machine-gun fire. Despite being wounded the pilot somehow managed to land again safely.

He also survived efforts, which began in 1972, by the Bishops of Kitium, Kyrenia, and Paphos to demand his resignation from the civil office of President of the Republic, on the grounds that it ran contrary to the laws of the Church of Cyprus.

On the 7 March 1973 the Bishops met and sentenced Makarios to be dethroned, and returned to the rank of layman. Shortly afterwards they went further and announced that Makarios was henceforth to be referred to as Michail Christodoulou Mouskos, a reference to his original birth-name.

In the end the three Bishops lost their own positions in July 1973 and were dethroned by the Supreme Holy Synod in Cyprus.

In the same period Makarios set up the Reservist Police Force, which became known simply as *'The Reservists'*. They were supported by hundreds of auxiliary police officers and its sole aim was to combat the activities of EOKA-B as the country slid closer to a virtual civil war.

By way of examples on 18 July 1973 fifty armed members of EOKA-B occupied Vatyli Police Station in broad daylight, in what was considered to be a dress rehearsal for *'Operation Apollo'* the coup plot. Eight days later General Grivas ordered the blowing-up of the Central Police Station in Limassol.

In one incident on the night of the 27 July 1973 Makarios supporters responded in a tit- for-tat exercise to bomb attacks by

EOKA-B, and by daylight sixty explosions had occurred in Limassol.

At times during this period Makarios struggled to maintain the political high ground as many Cypriots, a lot of young people among them, identified the aspirations of EOKA-B with that of the spirit of Enosis.

On the 7 October 1973 Makarios III survived another assassination attempt at Ayios Sergios in the Famagusta area, when a tarmacked area of a road he was due to travel through was blown up prematurely by an EOKA-B operative.

After the failed coup in 1974, where he managed to escape with the help of the British and left the island, Makarios eventually returned to Cyprus on 7 December 1974. He returned to Cyprus through the British Bases and was taken by helicopter from RAF Akrotiri to Nicosia.

Prior to his return elements of EOKA-B were still trying to discourage his return but a movement in Limassol called the *'National Rally'* gathered pace even though some referred to him as the *'Castro of the Mediterranean'*.

He re-assumed the presidency from Glafkos Clerides and addressed an estimated crowd of 250,000 people, who welcomed him home, from the balcony of the Archbishopric, which was still in ruins as a result of the coup.

During his speech he said, *"I was considered dead. Here I am alive."*

It was now time for Makarios to take stock of a divided country after the invasion, and ten days later he gave instructions to Clerides to begin talks with Turkish Cypriot leader Rauf Denktash on what has become universally known as the *'Cyprus problem'*.

The talks began in January 1975 and have continued to this day in one form or another.

***

(Andry):

"Maro had her second child Elizabeth or *'Lisa'* on the 25 April 1977 and she got her name from the mother of Kokos. The name Elizabeth was quite popular coming from the Queen of England as we had previously been under British occupation.

My sister Maro remembers how hard life was for her living at that house in Agios Athanasios – it was more than seven years before she had any electricity at all. She was devoted to bringing up her children with just one small diesel lamp to hang in the middle of the room, and a stove to cook and boil hot water for washing themselves and clothes.

They had no fridge, and the small room they lived in was divided by a cabinet in the middle, to separate the kitchen area and the sleeping area, where for a while everyone slept together.

In the winter at 6pm they went to bed, and in the summer at 9pm, as there was very little else to do. Her father-in-law had a small black and white TV which was about 6" x 6" in size and powered by batteries. If they gathered round to watch a film they couldn't guarantee to see the end because the batteries didn't last more than two hours.

Kokos was usually out every evening and wouldn't return until the early hours. At some stage Maro remembers that she found out that he was having an affair with a Lebanese woman who was working at their kiosk. That day she froze in her chair and never moved all day. Eventually her mother-in-law took her to a doctor's but would not get involved in what had gone on.

From that day Maro swore an oath to herself that she would never spend the day frozen to a chair in shock for this man again.

The very next day Kokos offered to buy her a swimming costume so that she could go swimming at the sea by the beach, something that he had never previously allowed her to do."

***

(Andry):

"In due course I moved to the new school.

It had been under construction for the previous couple of years. We were all so excited watching, and waiting, for it to be finished. It was huge compared to the two big classes of the old school. We couldn't wait to move. The new school was built on the top of the hill. There was nothing round it at that time, just wild bushes. I used to go there and play with my friends, or on a school day out.

With all the new families the old school was just not big enough. A small room was rented from a neighbour and used as a classroom. Then there was another room opposite the front gate. We used to be like eighty, to one hundred, students all together and spread in three classes.

At the end of every school year we had school activities with different sports competitions. I was very competitive and I wanted always to come first.

This particular year, before June 1977 we were hosting the sports-fair. All the villages around were coming to the new school, Akrotiri, Kolossi, Ypsonas, Asomatos, Erimi and our village Trachoni were participating. I was taking part in the running with obstacles. I was sure that I was going to come first within twelve competitions. But when the start was given I kept back for a couple of seconds and that was it - I came second and I was so disappointed!"

***

Makarios III, as he became known, died unexpectedly of a heart attack on 3 August 1977, ten days short of his 64th birthday.

In order to confirm the cause of death, Makarios's heart was removed during a post- mortem. The heart has since been preserved in his former bedroom in the Archbishopric.

He was buried in a tomb on the mountain of Throni, a site that he personally chose, near to Kykkos Monastery. Outside an inscription reads, *'Thousands of Makarios will continue your struggle.'*

Throni is 3 km from the monastery and at the entrance to the site is now a massive bronze statue 13 meters high, of Makarios, which used to be located in the Archbishops Palace in Nicosia.

The path leading to his tomb is lined with religious mosaics, and the entrance is guarded by Cypriot soldiers.

His funeral was held at St. John's Cathedral outside the Archbishopric in Nicosia and one hundred and eighty two dignitaries from fifty-two countries attended, whilst an estimated 250,000 mourners – about half of the Greek Cypriot population of the island, at the time, filed past the coffin.

Unusually for August in Cyprus it rained on the day and Greek Cypriots declared that they were *'tears from heaven'*.

(Andry):

"I went with my mother and father to the funeral and there were thousands of people queuing to pay their respects. I wasn't quite twelve years old and there were lots of people around me crying and very upset.

He was much loved by many people and a book was signed which was full of great condolences. Some people did say though that because he was a priest he was too forgiving instead of punishing those who went against him."

***

By way of example Makarios offered an amnesty to members of EOKA-B using the words, *'I offer to all an amnesty and remission of sins, in the hope that the desired harmony and unity of our people will follow',* but Nikos Sampson refused the offer and in 1977 he became the only person to be prosecuted for his involvement in the military coup.

He was sentenced to twenty years in prison, and two years later was granted parole. He then lived in France for eleven years before returning to Cyprus in 1990 where he served part of the remaining sentence and was freed again in 1993. Sampson died in 2001.

***

After the death of Archbishop Makarios a Cypriot politician by the name of Spyros Kyprianou became Acting President of the Cyprus Republic, in accordance with the constitution.

On the 3 September 1977 he was confirmed as the President and, after winning two further presidential elections in later years, he remained in post until 1988.

***

(Andry):

"I think it was my first year in the Gymnasium school in September 1977 when I started swimming at the Limassol Swimming Club with a friend named Maro. She was already an athlete, and a couple of years older than me, but I knew her through a common friend.

The club was quite a distance so I was travelling with the bus into Limassol and after getting off near to Ayia Napa church Maro was picking me up with her bicycle and we rode a few kilometres to get to the club.

We were swimming in the sea and after training we would do the same journey back in reverse. It was very tiring but I was determined to try to do other things.

At some point we started swimming in a pool but as the weather started to close in for the winter it got very difficult with the travelling and the distance was just too much.

Finally on one occasion I missed my last bus back to Trachoni and I walked all the way to my father's place at the port, where I found him, and he took me home.

He made it very clear to me however that he couldn't do that again and that was the end of it – no more swimming club.

We never had the means to do anything extra other than go to school. We had no way to communicate and no-one to drive us anywhere. The same thing happened when I was asked to do some training for running and athletics at Tsirion Stadium in Limassol. I just had no way of getting there.

The only exception to this was when I had some private lessons in the last year of elementary school when we started to learn English. My parents sent me to Limassol twice a week on the bus to Ayios Ioannis for some lessons. This was for me a luxury, as we were not used to spending money unnecessarily.

***

In the same year my father took all of the family to see a Russian ship in the port at Limassol.

Because he was working in the Customs there we were allowed access. It was huge and was called the *'Bella Russia'* and he took us for a walk all round it.

I remember that I was so impressed with the whole ship that I wrote an essay about it at school. My teacher and head-master of the school, Mr Mylonas, was impressed and said, *'You are going to be a writer Andry!'*

This book fulfils that prophecy!

***

Around this time we also accommodated some Palestinian orphaned children in our village. They were of our age group and were on some sort of trip. At some point my mother couldn't find her gold cross and thought that she had lost, or misplaced it.

Then our guest asked to buy a second suitcase, which my mother was surprised about because her first one was half-empty when she arrived.

One day when we were out she looked in Suchiras suitcase and with great disappointment she found her lost cross with the chain, with lots of other clothing and bedding that belonged to us. My mother took everything back and because they were soon leaving to go back to their country she decided not to make an issue of it.

Another Palestinian boy took a knife and threatened the boy of a family he was staying with because he wanted to use his bicycle – it was not a good experience after all!

Yet another childhood memory during this year was also in Trachoni village. I had a friend called Olympia and we used to go to school together. One afternoon we all gathered at her house to play and she gave everyone a piece of chocolate except me. I was very annoyed with her because she had left me out but after a while all of my friends started to go to the toilet. The chocolate was actually a laxative to help people with constipation!

That was supposed to be a big joke but it was a bad one!"

Figure 63 Schools Competitions – Andry front row far

left – wearing no. 3 for Trachoni village (1977)

Figure 64 Competition between schools – Andry far left

(1977)

Figure 65 Competition between schools – Andry front row far left (1977)

Figure 66 Lania Village - S.K. EDEK talk by Vasos Lissarides – Andry seated front row 2nd left facing the speaker (circa 1977)

Figure 67 Limassol – Palestinian children visiting (1977)

Figure 68 Limassol Harbour – on Sami's yacht – Andry front

left (1977

Figure 69 Paphos Port by the castle – Andry far right holding a swordfish (1977)

Figure 70 Sami/Roulla/Andrys mother/Michalis/Chrystalla/Despo/Andry – with Aphrodite's Rock in the background (1977)

Figure 71 School-friend Christos in centre of picture – Andry to the right holding nephew Kostas (circa 1977)

Figure 72 6th Grade Elementary School Trachoni Class Photo – Andry middle row second right - 1976/1977

Chapter Fourteen

1978

A Death In The Family

(Andry):

My grandfather Christodoulos (Takis) died in 1978.
He was retired but still did some work helping my uncle Telos at his business by the sea where they were excavating shingle for building purposes.

My grandfather was still living in Geroskipou when he suffered a second head-stroke. He loved his food with lots of salt and that day he had eaten sardines, which are very salty. Although he knew that he shouldn't take salt he refused to listen to doctors, or the family, as he just wanted to enjoy life up until his last moment.

They took him to a private doctor who told them to take him straight to Paphos hospital. He was in there for two weeks and never stood on his feet again.

Whilst he was in hospital my uncle Aristotelis stayed with him at his bedside. He finally left the hospital on the Saturday and died at home on the Monday morning. Moments like this make you realise how much you love your parents, you want to look after them, and see them stay alive for as long as possible.

There was a big funeral in the village and the service took place at Agia Paraskevi Church. My mother didn't take any of the children to the funeral, except for Michalis who was still very young.

After that we occasionally saw my step-grandmother Despinou, who would visit us in Trachoni. The roads were not very good between Paphos and Limassol and she never stayed the night as she preferred to get back to her own home. In those days she needed to take a taxi or a bus as other forms of transport were not good at all."

***

The first highway in Cyprus was not completed until October 1985 and was called the Cyprus A1. It connected Nicosia to Limassol and eventually was extended from Limassol to Paphos.

***

(Andry):

"During the summer that the school was closed I went to earn some money in a workshop where they made boxes for packing fruit. I was only helping to prepare the glue and then putting the labels on the boxes using a brush and dipping it into the glue. I was only there for three or four weeks but I saved my money and bought a yellow inflatable boat for us to use on the beach. It had a couple of oars with it and we had great fun with it in the sea.

***

When I was thirteen I had my first period, the day before we were due to go on a school trip. I didn't really know what to do and was too embarrassed and shocked to discuss it with my mother. My friend Mary showed me how to use what we called *'serviettes'* and that was it.

When I did finally tell my mother she smacked my face and it went red. I hadn't done anything wrong it was just an old custom to sort of wake you up from the shock of the event!

As I was growing up I was doing my share of the housework and one day whilst my mother was out I was looking after Michalis.

As I was finishing mopping the floor Michalis wanted to enter the house with mud on his shoes. The floor was still wet so I closed the door and left him outside. He banged the door and shouted to me but I wasn't prepared to let him in.

Not to be outdone he went around the side of the house, smashed a small window, to open the catch, and climbed in.

At the end of the day it was no surprise that I got the blame for it – Michalis was always innocent and never to blame. Even to this day he occupies a special place in my mother's eyes!

***

On the 19 December 1978 my sister Roulla gave birth to her first child Lina. She was such a beautiful baby and as her aunties we all looked after her."

Figure 73 Governors Beach – Andry far left (1978)

Figure 74 Costas/Andry/Despo/Chrystalla (1978)

Chapter Fifteen

1979

'Lefkoma' – The Book Of Memories

(Andry):

"On the 2 March 1979 I completed an entry in my *'Lefkoma'* my *'Book Of Memories'* as follows, *'To my dear friends and people that I know. Please write a few words for me so that I can remember you. With love Andry.'*

Over a period of the following months my friends from the 9th Gymnasium and Lycium school, which was at Ayios Antonios, in the Turkish area of Limassol, between the Old and New Ports, completed entries in the book, as well as some members of my family.

Not yet fourteen years of age we were already pre-occupied with thoughts of husbands and success.

The hopes and aspirations within the following messages still hold true to this day:

Despo (sister) – 3.3.1979 – *'Written a beautiful night – When your beautiful hair they blow against the sun and your hazelnut eyes they're looking the nature, you look like a flower untouched which starts to blow and spread love.'*

Despo Costa Christou subsequently married and had four children, two sons and two daughters. She later divorced and still lives in Trachoni, where she still loves nature, is a vegetarian, and is skilled at painting religious icons as well as other artwork.

***

Stavroulla Christoforou - (school-friend from Limassol) – *'My dear friend Andry. Me who knows what you are asking from the world what you are looking. I wish you to get married the boy that you adore. With love your friend.'*

***

Panayiota Christofi - (school-friend from Trachoni) – *'My dear friend Andry I wish the ship of your young dreams to embark one day to the port of joy, friendship and to eternal happiness.'*

Panayiota married her boyfriend from school, Kyriacos Christodolou, who was one year older than her. He is now the *'muhktar'*, community leader, of Trachoni village and they have three children.

Also known as Yiota, she has spoken recently about her memories of Andry, *'I remember you always as a good friend. We played together in the neighbourhood but always you were helping me with mathematics because you were very good. The other thing was that whatever you put in your mind you were doing it. And now I'm telling you that you are going to succeed in what you are doing. You were a fighter and a very good girl. A good friend and above all else you were a very good student!'* (15.3.2017)

***

Constantina Constantinou – (school-friend) – 21.3.1979 – *'Destiny separates people and leaves leave the branches. Each one sees new worlds but the heart doesn't change. I wish you my Andry your life to be like Mathematics. Your joy to be plus and your sorrow to be minor. With love...'*

Constantina is now married and has children. She lives near Trachoni village.

***

Christos Jampou – (school-friend) – *'My dear school-mate Andry. Everybody's writing to you poems coming out from books. I have only three wishes for you. Wealth, Joy and Health. Also I wish you a good career to your life and everything you wish to come true. It's written a morning in April.'*

I believe that Christos is now a mathematics teacher and that he lives in Limassol.

***

Lefki Onisiforou – (school-friend) – 14.3.1979 – *'This is written a beautiful morning in March. My dear friend Andry I wish you with all my heart to find happiness in life, the pain and the sorrow never to know. With all my love your friend and schoolmate'.*

Lefki was a very close friend of mine who now lives in Zakaki near Limassol. She married and has two children. She works in a beauty shop.

Lefki has more of her memories of school-life recorded within the book.

***

John Onisforou – (cousin of Lefki) – *'Andry I wish you a good career in your life and a happy future, and I wish you to live a life that people will envy.'*

John was not in my school but at some point he was a friend.

***

Demetris Kakoulla - (school-friend- a refugee from Leonariso in Famagusta) – *'Written at night at 1.30am on the 1.4.1979. Me that I know what you're asking in the world, what you are looking, I wish you to get married the boy you adore. With love your schoolmate. Love light, love life, love the world.'*

***

Pantelis Panteli – (school-friend) – *'My dear schoolmate Andry I wish you to live a happy life and that people envy your life and everything you desire soon to happen. Live life and love a man that is capable.'*

***

Pola – (female school-friend) – *'Dear Andry if you want my friend to know what I have in secret turn and see the capitals they have the secret that I have hidden in my heart. Oh here is the secret. SAGAPO – I love you.'*

***

Lucas Louka – (school-friend) – *'My dear schoolmate Andry – I wish you to fulfil your dreams to marry a boy you adore. Dream dreams beautiful.'*

***

Michael Michalakis – (school-friend) – 3 May 1979 - *'My dear schoolmate Andry I wish you whatever you wish to come true and to live life happy and admired by people with the boy that you love. Love a man capable.'*

***

Irene Petrou – (school-friend) – *'My Andry I wish you a good career in your life together with three wishes. Wealth, Joy and Health.'*

***

Stavros Arestis – (school-friend who lived in Akrotiri village) – written lunchtime on 10.4.1979 – *'My dear schoolmate Andry. I wish you to fulfil all your dreams and I wish you a good career and to your studies. As well I wish you three wishes, Health, Joy and Wealth.'*

***

Georgos Kourouzos – (school-friend) – *'My dear schoolmate Andry I wish you a good career in your life and happy future. Live life.'*

He went on to do computer studies and I once met him years later when I went into a computer shop where he was the manager. He recognised me but I didn't recognise him straight away!

***

Sami Al Addin – (my sister Roulla's husband) – 2.3.1979 - *'I hope for you the best and to get all your dreams.'*

***

Mohamed Ala Addin – (younger brother of Sami) – *'Andri 'B' you used to call me 'Paticha' for a nickname which means water-melon. I came from Palestine, came and stayed for a while. If you want to live a good life you must love everything and anything.'*

***

Maria Pavlou – (school-friend) – *'My Andry life is sweet but full of needles. Tell yourself not to look back because your eyes will go wet and you will deeply get hurt. Don't take life seriously but always to enjoy it and be happy. I wish the boat of your life to embark in the port that's called love.'*

***

Kyriakos Pahipis – (school-friend) – *'What shall I write to you Andry songs and flowers and green horses (bullshit) I don't know. Our life is so little and we want to do many things to enjoy and live it. I wish you then if really the wishes can come true a life with happiness and the dreams that you dream to come true. I wish you this with all my heart.'*

I met Kyriakos once when he was doing his national service as a sailor in the navy by the Old Port. Later on he owned a bookshop somewhere near Tsirion Football Stadium, along with his wife, and also got a job in a bank.

***

Anthi Petrou – (school-friend) – *'My dear schoolmate Andry. In a garden I will go and flowers I will pick for you and your golden album I will make it with flowers like a wreath. But again I thought that a good wish will be better than the flowers. And the wish I will say is to be happy, the pain and the sorrow never to know.'*

***

Georgos Pantouris – (school-friend from Linopetra) – *'My dear schoolmate I wish you with all my heart to find happiness in life to live life happy, with joy and find a man as worth it to marry and to share together the joy of life.'*

I believe that Georgos became a talent scout looking for good football players.

***

Sotiroulla Andreou Panayiotou – (school-friend) – *'My dear friend and schoolmate Andry. I'll enter into the garden to choose flowers for your album to decorate it but still I thought that a good wish is better from all the flowers. With endless love...'*

***

Roulla – (sister to Andry) – Sunday 13 May 1979 at 2.45pm – *'Remember we were sitting with Mohamed and my mother-in-law. Andry I wish you one day that you will go through this album to see and to have happy memories and to remember me as I will remember you always wherever we are. Now I wish you to make a good career and a happy family and to live as many years you wish. With love always from your sister Irene!'*

My sister went on to have three children with her first husband Sami but eventually divorced. She later got remarried and lives in Trachoni in the house which was built above my mothers.

Some of her words were to come true many years later as I re-read the book as part of my research.

***

Marios – (cousin and son of my father's brother Vassos) – *'I'd just decided to come down, all the way from London Town, I only really came back, to wish you lots of love and luck. With best wishes for the future, your loving cousin Mario'*

15 May 1979 from Marios and wife Soulla – *'To our dear Andry we wish you now that you are on the sweet excitements of your school life not to get drift from the waves and the weeds of life but to keep your ego high and your self-confidence with determination and patience for sure you will reach the point of happiness that every young one desires. We wish you from our heart to fulfil every sweet dream. Happy days. A good career and good fortune. With our warmest wishes and love.'*

My cousin Marios runs a very successful restaurant in the tourist area of Germasoyia in Limassol called *'The Shakespeare'*. His first marriage with Soulla failed at some point and he later remarried. He has three children from his first marriage, two sons and a daughter.

***

Pavlou Kostakis Andreou – (school-friend and a refugee from Arsos in Larnaca) – *'Written one night of April at 11pm. My dear schoolmate Andry. I wish you from my heart to get the man you love and never to cry. As well I wish you to pass the road of life with joy and happiness.'*

***

Maria Yangou – (school-friend from Limassol) – Wednesday 9.5.1979 – *'My dear friend and schoolmate Andry. The mum who gave birth to you golden to be her heart. That makes a daughter so beautiful that shines in the neighbourhood. I wish you from the bottom of my heart a good success on your studies and everything you wish to have it with endless and forever love...'*

***

Despo – (friend) – *'Dear friend Andry if you want to know what I have in my heart read the capitals they will tell you the truth the secret that I have in my heart how much I want to tell*

you.....SAGAPO – I love you.'

***

Isabella Savvidou – (school-friend and a refugee from Ammochostos Famagusta) – *'Written one night of March at 10pm. My dear schoolmate Andry I wish you from the bottom of my heart a good career in your life and to fulfil all your desires.'*

Isabella got married and lives in Limassol. I believe that she has one child and we met once when I was demonstrating some products at a house.

***

Anthoulla Xeni – (my best-friend *'koumera'*) – 16.3.1979 – *'My Andry the years pass quickly and life is passing by and only this album stays when we are old. And then when you go through the pages one by one you will remember your friends and remember me as well. With love.'*

Anthoulla married her boyfriend from school who died in a road accident. She has two sons who are both excellent swimmers.

She was the main bridesmaid at my first wedding and baptised my son Marios. We still keep in touch and today she lives in Erimi.

***

Flora Vassiliou – (school-friend from Ayios Ioannis in Limassol) – *'My Andry I wish you good career in your life and together with that Im writing for you three wishes, Wealth, Happiness, and Health.'*

***

Pantelitsa Leonidou – (school-friend from Trachoni) – *'My Andry – when the Greek denies the desire for Greece only then I will deny you my dear friend. Within the years of life that you are going to live I wish you wealth, happiness and health. Never misery and pain. With lots of love your friend – Courage - Determination – Coolness – Patience.'*

***

Olga Stavrou – (school-friend) – Written one afternoon of 15.3.1979 Day Thursday at 9pm) – *'My dear friend Andry I wish you good career and a good fulfilment of your wishes and desires. With*

endless love...'

I grew up with Olga from the age of six years. She married and had four children. She still lives in Trachoni and all of her children have done very well. One of her daughters studied at a university in Birmingham. Her husband is a coach and does PE in schools.

Olga never went to work; she was always a housewife and looked after her family.

***

Margarita Pourikkou – (school-friend and a refugee from Agios Sergios in Famagusta) – *'My Andry everyone writes you poems coming out from books. I wish you Health, Happiness and Wealth. With love...'*

She got married with her boyfriend from school and owned a travel agency. I think that she had two sons. She originally came from the same village as my former husband.

***

Roulla Mavri – (My first-cousin and daughter of Uncle Yiannis from Nicosia) –21.6.1979 – *'Written one night. To my beloved Andry I wish you every happiness and joy in your life and every dream to come true. In life you will have to deal with lots of obstacles within the many joys. Don't get desperate. Don't walk back. Keep going.*

Fight and you will see that you will succeed at the end. Life is beautiful as long as you know how to live it....'

***

Some people might find it strange that even at such a young age we were so focussed on settling down with husbands. The priority for women in those days was to get married and to have children. The boys were the ones who were expected to have careers.

I once said to my father that I wanted to go to a disco and his answer was to say that when I got engaged my fiancée would take me. The only escape was for us to get engaged. You couldn't just have a boyfriend and go out – it just wasn't allowed.

My father's attitude was best that we got married and followed our lives - it was a man's world!

When my father saw my sister Roulla was struggling at school he took her out and sent her to sewing classes so she did not finish her education. That was his way of trying to give her a skill that she could use later in life.

My sister actually heard my parents discussing the matter beforehand and decided never to go back to school again!

***

I had a schoolmate called Gavriella in the second grade at the Gymnasium who was attacked by someone with a knife as she was going home from school.

She was living in the Ayios Ioannis area and was walking home when this happened. She was having an affair with an older boy who was aged eighteen, to nineteen years, and the year after they got engaged she left school. She was still thirteen but she had the body of an eighteen year old.

She was a very beautiful girl, slim with long brown hair, dark skin and green eyes. I think she made people jealous because of that.

***

During the summer school holidays, which were usually in July and August, I wanted to earn some money. This was only for my personal expenses and to try to get things like clothes and shoes, as we were always short of them. We couldn't afford a lot and always we needed more.

If I remember well when I was thirteen years old, and also the year after, I worked at Lanitis Packing House. I don't remember how I used to get there but I think that there was a bus to pick up all the workers from the village and transfer them to the workplace.

Lanitis was a very well known plantation, by Fassouri Water Park, and people from most of the local villages were working there. A lot of them were using bicycles as they were too poor to own a car.

The packing house was a big high building with just the roof made with iron and aluminium. There were lots of rows of tables and the packing women were sat in the middle of the tables filling big wooden boxes of grapes, before they went onto a pallet.

Two other women were sitting to the side of the tables clipping the grapes and cleaning the ones that weren't good. Then these were placed very gently into wooden boxes and when they were full a boy would pick them up and pile them somewhere else.

When a pallet was full, a forklift truck would be used to pick it up and take it to a storage area, or into a big fridge, before being taken off to the port at Limassol for export.

It was all very well organised and every Friday we got paid which we looked forward to very much. Much of my money went on new school uniforms and a bag but I had no complaints.

It was tiring but we had a laugh as well. I remember that I kept saying that when I got married I wanted to have four children, two boys and two girls and I wanted twins as well.

At the time I didn't know that much of my dreams would come true. By the age of twenty-seven years I had three boys and a girl, and my two youngest were born on the same day with two years between them, so I almost had it exactly.

Because of what I wanted the women at the packing house were giving me the double grapes in order to help me have twins in the future. It was a silly thing but it was kind of believed by many people.

My friend Anthoulla was working there too. Her mother Mrs Ellada, which means Greece, was cooking in the kitchen there for the managers and owners of the place. Every lunch- break they were sitting at long tables and eating what she cooked for the day. She had a couple of regular options - lentil beans, and black beans.

On the 15 December 1979 my sister Maro gave birth to her third child who was named Loukia after my mother.

Figure 75 Trachoni – Despo/Andry holding her niece

Lina/Michalis (1979)

Figure 76 Troodos – family gathering – Andry far left at rear

(circa 1979)

Figure 77 Troodos – family gathering – Andry far left at rear

(circa 1979)

Figure 78 Picture of Andry in her *'best wishes'* book (2.3.1979)

Chapter Sixteen

1980

Breaking Point

(Andry):

"In all these years I saw my parents fall out quite often. In some cases my father was just leaving our home to come back sometime after, maybe days, or weeks, whilst life was going on.

We were all as a family suffering with the whole situation but it wasn't under our control.

My mother always stayed strong and looked after us. Her aim was for us to become self- sufficient adults and independent. She never thought of her own personal happiness. Deep inside she loved my father, as my father loved her, but love alone doesn't lead to happiness always.

I love both my parents and respect them for what they bring to my life with no judgement being passed. They both did their best with what they knew, and still do. In their efforts to do the right thing in life they made mistakes that hurt each other.

When marriages break up in Cyprus divorce is a bit more complicated. You get married in church, and at the same time sign papers for a civil marriage, so you have to take papers for a civil divorce, and then a church divorce, where a panel of priests listen to the reasons for divorce before agreeing to it. You have to show reasonable grounds and sometimes the priests delay things if they think that the couple can sort their problems out. It is the Bishop who gives final approval.

***

I was also strong like my mother and when I decided to do something nothing would stop me.

One day during this time I remember going to a shop and seeing a classical guitar which I fell in love with. It was twenty-eight Cyprus pounds, which was a lot of money in those days but I was determined to have it and saved my money until I could buy it.

***

On 11 March 1980 my sister Roulla gave birth to her second child Sami."

***

(Andry):

"I think it was on the 26 April 1980 that my friend Lefki hosted a party at her home for her birthday. I remember having lots of fun and dancing to the 'rock and roll' song *'Funky Town'* which was one of my favourite songs.

This was song by the American disco act *'Lipps Inc'* from their debut album *'Mouth to Mouth'* in 1979, which was released as an album lead single in 1980.

There were lots of school-friends at the party and members of Lefki's family and it was a great success. I remember Lefki's mother Eleni who was so nice and kind, and very beautiful as well. Unfortunately she died a few years later from cancer.

Lefki's elder sister Charoulla was also there looking very beautiful. My friend Lefki was, and still is a very beautiful person, both inside and out."

***

(Andry):

"On the 21 June 1980 my mother's brother Telos died in an accident whilst he was at work. My uncle's quarry was by the beach before you reach Geroskipou village. As you come from Limassol there was a turning towards the place.

One day he had loaded his vehicle with shingle but as he and his driver started to leave they heard a noise from the lorry and Telos got out and went behind it to look to see what the problem was.

For some reason the driver moved backwards whilst my uncle was at the back and he was hit by the lorry, which knocked him over, and then ran over his body. As my uncle shouted the driver then moved forwards but in doing so ran over Telos again for a second time.

He was still alive and they managed to get him to the General Hospital at Paphos but he died the same day. Even after giving him seventeen bottles of blood they just couldn't stop the bleeding and he died from an uncontrolled haemorrhage.

My mother didn't manage to get to him to see him before he died.

The funeral was held at Agia Paraskevi Church in Geroskipou – the same church where my parents were married, I was christened, and the funeral service of my grandfather Takis was held a couple of years before.

Telos was buried alongside his father in the village cemetery.

Years later when my aunt Kyriakou (his wife) died, the family removed the bones of Telos from his grave and placed them with his wife. Finally they were together again.

My mother didn't take any of us to the funeral and we stayed home with our grandmother Irinou.

A couple of months before Telos died one of his daughters Stella got married and they had a baby. Following the death of Telos they decided to call the child Aristodelina after him. It was a beautiful baby girl with long eye-lashes but unfortunately after about three months the child got a lung infection and died – yet another family tragedy.

On the 12 October 1980 my sister Chrystalla got married at a church in Limassol, and Michalis was a page-boy at the wedding. Afterwards she went to live in a small house behind her parents-in-law and worked in a shipping office for a while.

***

When Michalis came along my sister Despo was always fighting with him because as the previous youngest child she still wanted the attention. It seems that we all behaved in this way as each new member of the family came along.

We didn't know when Michalis was born that he was going to be such a cheeky little boy. He was mostly spoiled as he was the only boy in the family. I always tried to protect him and look after him.

Michalis remembers fighting with Despo over minor things but always he tried to make sure that she got the blame! On one occasion he scratched his own arms with his fingernails, to the point where he drew blood. Then he started crying and screaming. My mother responded to his call at which point Michalis accused Despo of doing it.

Despite protesting her innocence my mother shouted at Despo and gave her a few smacks – how dare she harm her little brother and then try to claim that she was innocent!

Whilst my mother was telling her not to do it again Michalis was standing behind her smiling – he had achieved what he wanted!

Figure 79 Curium Amphitheatre – Andry (1980)

Figure 80 Trachoni – Andry far left/her nephew

Sami/Lina/Andry's mother Loukia (1980)

Figure 81 Wedding of cousin Stella in Paphos – Andry to the left of the bride and Telos to the right in the year of his death in 1980

Figure 82 Pinou – dressed in black at Stella's wedding in 1980

Figure 83 Andry holding Lina at Throni – Tomb of Makarios –

1980

Figure 84 Photo of Stella with her father Telos, and mother

Kyriacou (in red) at her wedding – 1980

Chapter Seventeen

1981

Tragedy & Engagement

(Andry):

"Sunday 15th of February 1981 and I remember it was a rainy day. We left together with my father, just me and him, for Nicosia in the early morning. There was a conference of S.K EDEK, *(Social Club United Democratic Greeks of Cyprus),* the political party of my father, which we were going to attend.

I didn't really understand much about politics, and politicians, but my father did, and when it was close to elections we used to go out at night putting posters on the poles and walls for the Party, as part of an election campaign.

***

The President of EDEK was Vassos Lyssarides, who was an MP, and the party was founded in 1969. It was the first socialist party to be founded in Cyprus.

Vassos Lyssarides was born in 1920 and after Independence from the British was declared he became an important political figure. On the 30 August 1974 an attempt was made on his life during which an EDEK youth leader was killed, namely Doros Loizou.

Doros was driving a vehicle, with his wife sat next to him, and Lyssarides was in the back seat when they were ambushed by 'fascists'.

Doros was shot but managed to accelerate away to safety before being overcome by his injuries and dying.

He is remembered for saving the lives of the others by his actions.

When my sister Chrystalla got married to Tasos his best-man was Vassos Lyssarides.

***

Anyway, wherever there was a speech of the political president of my father's party, we were following. It was a way for me as well to get out from home, as we were not allowed to go out next to nothing, or to see friends during the weekends. Both of my parents were very strict as to where we went and that included all of my sisters.

My elder sister Maro fell in love at the age of thirteen-and-a-half, with a sixteen year-old boy, and ended up at the age of seventeen getting married, and had her first child soon after.

My second sister Erini got married at the age of eighteen, after falling in love with a friend of my father's, who was twelve years older.

My third sister Chrystalla got married, at the age of twenty years, with another friend of my father's Tasos, who belonged to the same political party. He really loved my sister, so he asked for her hand in marriage. It worked out successfully for them.

And then it was me at the age of fifteen, still a teenager, with my worries in life, and my dreams and hopes. So, my father was quite careful where I was going and whom I saw or met. And my mother was much stricter as she said, living in a village without relatives close to have an eye on us, she was always worrying if anyone might abuse or touch us. So we had no nights out, or school parties of friends, or meets after school. So whenever there was an opportunity for a day out anywhere, with my father, or all the family, it was fantastic for me.

Anyway we attended this conference and on the way back we had a flat tyre. My father changed it with the spare one and just before the traffic lights at Limassol New Port there was a garage open. So he stopped to fix the flat tyre. I felt tired and cold, as it was winter, and it was raining a bit, so I decided to stay in the car, as my father stepped out to go to speak to the mechanic.

As I was waiting and looking round I noticed a big black bike in the garage being propped up obviously for some kind of repair.

That attracted my attention as I liked big bikes, and I decided to jump out of the car to have a closer look.

A young man was standing close by and talking with the mechanic and my father about the bike. I assumed that it was his bike and that he was there for the same reason we were. I paid a good look at him and I felt excited thinking of him riding that big Suzuki 1000 cc bike!

He looked quite young but he was obviously old enough to ride. He had long very curly light brown hair, brown to green eyes, and a heavily tanned skin. He was talking about looking to go to Greece to bring back some parts for the bike as they were not able to find them in Cyprus.

I tried to get into a conversation with him and tried to give an indication as to where my school was, because I liked him - I actually liked him and I wanted to see him again. So the way to see him again was for him to come to my school!

Anyway I left with my father, after leaving the car tyre to be fixed, and the romance was gone as fast as it started. Just silly me having silly ideas as I was a teenager and everything looked over and above the reality. But two weeks later there he was in the school-yard, on the bike, speaking to a student.

My face lit up and I said to my close-friend Lefki, *"That's him, that's the boy I was talking to you about, he is here, what do you think?"* Lefki paid a good look and she turned round to me with a funny face, *"Is this the person you like; I don't believe you!! Look at his hair, it's like a schesto!!!"*

'Schesto' is a traditional big round tray made from straw for carrying the bread on and she laughed generously!!

I said to her, *"I like him, he is handsome, there's nothing wrong with his hair! And he is riding a big bike!! I like his bike!! I'm going to speak to him."*

And I started walking towards him. So, what was I going to say to him; my friend hurried to walk next to me. I decided I would ask him if he had been to Greece to get the bikes parts.

Before Lefki could say anything I was there standing close! I said hello, and asked him if he had been to Greece yet, to get the parts he needed for the bike. He looked at me for a second and then smiled indicating that he recognised me - I think!!

His name was Christakis and he told me that arrangements had been made to send them to Cyprus, so he wouldn't need to go.

"Oh that's better really isn't it....." - I was trying to keep a conversation going and I had no clue what to say!

Afterwards Christakis began visiting the school at different times and I was always trying to say a hello and show myself in front of him.

Lefki was my very good friend and we had some great times together. She remembers one occasion when she planned a *'pretend fight'* with my other friend Lydia in order not to have the lesson. Lefki put Lydia's bag under her desk and when the teacher came in Lydia started shouting and asking where her bag was. Then she pretended to find the bag and they started to scream and pull each other's hair, and fall on the floor. By the time the teacher had parted them the lesson time was over.

***

Two weeks after a big tragedy happened ending with three deaths and lots of people being injured.

Two days after that accident Christakis ended up in the hospital after being involved in a traffic accident on his bike."

***

On Saturday March 14 1981 the Cyprus Mail reported in the following terms, *'Three Greek Cypriot schoolgirls were killed, and forty-eight other persons, including four teachers were injured, some of them seriously, when their bus collided with a passenger car, fell into a cliff, and plunged into a small dam, about twenty miles from Limassol yesterday afternoon.*

The accident happened when boys and girls from the Limassol Economic Lyceum were on their way to an excursion with their teachers to the Troodos hills.

One of the buses, driven by Cleanthis Georgiou of Akrotiri collided with a passenger car driven by an alien on the sloping road near Moniatis village about twenty miles from Limassol.

The bus fell into a cliff about forty feet deep and then plunged into a small dam.

The alarm was immediately given and rescue teams and ambulances were sent from Limassol.

The three girls found dead in the bus were Vassiliki Charalambous of Akrotiri, Anastasia Panayi of Limassol, and Ekaterini Strati of Trachoni.

As one of the ambulance vehicles was returning to Limassol with one of the three girls it came into collision with a vehicle of the British Bases and the two men on the rescue team were injured and so was the driver of the British Bases vehicle.

By last night thirty of the injured boys and girls and their teachers were detained at Limassol hospital for treatment, the others having been released after first-aid treatment.

The driver of the bus had his arm amputated.

The Minister of Education last night visited the injured teachers and students at Limassol hospital.

Immediately news came about the accident President Kyprianou got in touch with the various services for information and to convey his condolences to the casualties and their families.

The President is going to Limassol today, together with the
Minister of Health to visit the casualties at Limassol hospital and to
convey his regrets personally to the families of the victims.'

***

(Andry):

"It was March 1981 and we were due to have a school day
out. The whole school was going all over Cyprus to different
destinations. I was in the 1st year of Lyceum and my class consisted
of only girls - thirty-four of us all together. I was normally number
thirty-three because of my surname. In the Greek alphabet the letter
'c' is an 'x' which means I was nearly last."

***

Larnaca is the oldest town in Cyprus and features a 16th Century
fort, and a 9th Century church when the Phoenicians founded a
kingdom. The Church of Saint Lazarus is to be found there.

The Mycenaean Greeks fortified the town in the 12th
century, and today's city is the site of the kingdom of Kition which

355

is also the birthplace of the philosopher Zeno. Larnaca is the third largest city in Cyprus on the southern coast.

Before the invasion the port of Famagusta handled 80% of general cargo through Cyprus but from 1975 the economy of Larnaca grew as it sought to cope with some of that capacity, as entry to Famagusta was denied by the Turkish army.

***

(Andry):

"In the days before the trip we were talking about visiting Larnaka, Finikoudes. It was a popular place to visit by the sea. It had a long road alongside the beach with lots of palm trees and a lot of cafes and restaurants on the other side. The same day we were supposed to visit some archaeological sites, one being an old Turkish mosque on the west of the salt lake, and generally get to know and improve our knowledge about our country."

***

Just outside Larnaca, next to the salt lake, and near to the airport, is the *'Hala Sultan Tekke'*, an important Muslim pilgrimage site, ranking after sites such as the shrines at Mecca, Medina and Al Aqsa in Jerusalem.

In the 7th century the Arabs started raiding Cyprus and during one of these attacks Umm Haram, *(Respected Mother),* a relative of the Prophet Mohammed, fell from her mule and died in 647 AD. She was buried at the spot where she died and later the Turks built the present mosque in her honour. The shrine is also known as the *'Tekke of Umm Haram'.*

Every year the salt lake fills with water during the winter season and thousands of flamingo birds feed there between November and March.

***

(Andry):

"We were all so excited that morning. Everyone tried to dress casually and comfortable, but nice at the same time. We were taking with us enough money, or whatever our parents could afford to give us to spend. Most of us had a little bag with us containing chocolates, snacks and water.

There was a bit of a panic during that morning as the teachers were trying to put every class on the right bus. I can't remember how many buses that were parked in the yard of the 9th Lyceum School that tragic Friday the 13th.

Eventually we were sorted and all the students were sat on a bus waiting to leave. Suddenly a teacher came inside ours and said, "Everybody out of this bus, you are using that bus over there."

Nobody was happy as we did like the new big bus. We all complained and the answer was that they wanted the new bus to take the 2nd class of Lyceum to the mountains and we would be fine with an old bus. The road to Larnaca was just straight whereas the roads to the mountain were not so easy to drive on.

At that moment we had no idea what was going to happen. We were just upset that they had changed our bus, but we had no option other than to do as we were told.

On the way to Larnaca we were singing, chatting, eating and we were all very happy having this relaxing day for us other than spending it in the class doing lessons!! But everything was gone and the smile and happiness disappeared from our faces with the tragic radio news:

'A bus full of school children from the 9th Lyceum School has been in an accident on the way to Troodos mountains. Still there is no further information as to how many are injured!'

We all went speechless for few seconds looking at each other and then the fear and the look of desperation *'apognosi'* was the picture on our faces. We had no clue which bus was that, or what really had happened. We had no mobile phones to contact anybody. The only way to find out more was the radio but there was not enough detail.

The journey back to school was the longest I can ever remember. The minute we were left there we all ran to Limassol General Hospital to see what exactly had happened. It was only more or less two miles away.

There was such a lot of confusion there and lots of people had gathered trying to find out who was in the bus that crashed. Was it my son; was it my daughter - the information coming out was not clear as to which class was in that bus.

My family were panicking as well. My brother-in-law and my sisters came to the hospital in their efforts to find out if I was okay. The days that followed were like a living nightmare. I thought I had lost my best friend because that class was her class. But she was so lucky. She didn't go with her class. She didn't go with any class. She stayed secretly behind to spend the day with her boyfriend by a park. That saved her life!

The *'Time Machine Magazine'* (Cyprus Edition) also reported on the accident under the title *'The brakes, the brakes'* describing the location of the accident as *'the turn of death'* and gave details of how one of the teachers had saved many lives.

Their article described how the students of the 9th Gymnasium of Limassol were sat on the back seats of the bus singing and happy that they were free from the stress of school for the day. Suddenly they felt the bus pick up speed going downhill and the laughter stopped abruptly.

One student reported that prior to the accident a teacher had mentioned that there was a problem with the brakes on the bus but that there was nothing to worry about and that the driver was going to stop the bus.

Near to Platres and more specifically close to the estate known as *'Monte Moniatis'* the bus was travelling very fast as the driver struggled to bring the vehicle under control.

Some of the children started screaming and others shouted *'the brakes'* as it hit a car being driven by a British person. At a point, where previous accidents had occurred, it then went over the cliff and fell into the water tank which was full of water inside.

The article went on to describe how, as students and teachers began to drown inside, one of the teachers saved a number of lives.

Takis Elepheriou was a PE teacher and taught at the Gymnasium. I knew him and remember him being a strong built man, not very tall, and dark-skinned. He looked quite tough but he was a very good teacher.

His wife Rena was also our PE teacher and was on the bus as well at the time. I knew her as well. She was slim build and very kind. All the students loved her very much.

They had a son Eleftherios who was at school with me in the same class for three years until I went into an all-girls class in the 4th grade to focus on secretarial training.

Anyway as the bus fell into the tank Takis Elepheriou was thrown out from a window and was injured. Despite this he jumped onto the side of the bus and started doing his best to save people. He took out the driver and Rena his wife and together they made efforts to pull out injured children.

Some of the teachers were later honoured for their rescue efforts.

Other students were breaking windows with whatever they could find and trying to get help. I was told later that at one point one of the girls that drowned was waving an arm out of one of the windows but they couldn't pull her out because she was stuck between the seats.

The article went on to describe how the three girls who drowned were finally pulled from the bus twenty minutes after the collision.

Later at the hospital in Limassol witnesses reported hearing the cries of desperation and crying as families and friends gathered in large numbers, not knowing at that stage who was among the dead and injured.

***

(The 'turn of death' has continued to live up to its reputation over the years. On the 20 November 1989 eight British soldiers were killed when their military vehicle lost control and went over the cliff. Ten years later on the 30 January 2000 a number of Sri Lankan and Filipino workers on a day trip were returning to Nicosia from Troodos when they were involved in an accident.

Their vehicle was overloaded and as the brakes overheated the driver lost control as the vehicle gathered speed and hit some side barriers. Six people lost their lives and a number of the injured suffered injuries requiring amputations.)

***

At the same time, just two days after the road accident at Moniatis, Christakis had an accident as well, and ended up being injured and operated on in the hospital.

On Sunday the 15th March 1981, at 8.15 am, Christakis had an accident with his bike and had surgery on his right leg. Pins were put in to keep the bones together. I didn't know immediately about it. A friend of his, Panikos Panayides, came to school on the Monday and said to me that the man with the big bike was in hospital after having had an accident.

Who was to know that four years later on Friday 15 March, at 8.15am, I was going to deliver our first son Valentinos at a private clinic in Limassol?

I was very upset when I heard the news and with the first opportunity I ran to the hospital to see him. That was the start of our relationship, because every day I had to run to the hospital after school, spend some time with him, give him some company, and take the next bus home.

***

The funeral of the girls didn't take long to happen - it was on Monday 16 March 1981.

My friend Andry Ioannou remembers that the funeral service for all three took place in the same church in Limassol and that some students from the other classes were carrying the coffins.

My friend Alekos was a cousin to two of the girls and even now he finds it hard to come to terms with the accident which could have been even worse if the coach had carried on rolling down the cliff.

In Cyprus we always do the funeral, if not the same day, the day after mostly because of the hot weather. Sometimes it can take longer if relatives are expected from abroad.

Katerina's funeral was so tragic. There was nobody that didn't cry for her loss. She was the fourth child of five, and she was so quiet and a very polite girl, very beautiful as well. She had dark skin, and dark brown hair, with hazelnut eyes. She was also a very good student. Her younger sister Panayiota was in my class from the first year at school until the third year in the Gymnasium.

After the accident the theology teacher we had at school, did a strange thing. He said that losing the three girls in the bus accident was a sign, so he decided to raise our scores for our final examination marks by three points. So if someone had got sixteen, out of twenty, they got nineteen out of twenty. If you had got eighteen points he said that he would owe a point for the next term.

***

I continued to see Christakis in the hospital for the whole time he stayed there, which was three weeks or more.

After that he was coming to see me at the school during my breaks and we used to sit by the side of the football ground, which was attached to the school.

He was walking with crutches for a while but that didn't stop him from seeing me.

I remember visiting his sister-in-law Roulla, who was married with his elder brother, and they were living just outside the school in the Turkish Cypriot area. They had just had a new born baby named Michalis and I got him a small teddy bear from Giorgalettes shop for a present.

Michalis was a beautiful 'chubby' baby and I loved him from the first moment.

I remember at the end of the school year, around June, after finishing our exams, Christakis took me on his bike and we spent a few hours at Curium beach. It was a nice day out but a secret one.

This was the nature of things in those days.

During the summer months Christakis was often riding past our house on his bike, to see if he could see me, and my mother started to notice this and to wonder who he was; in fact she even threatened to throw some water over him if he saw him too close to the house.

One day I left the house and jumped into a car which Christakis was driving. One of the villagers saw me get in and after we drove off he later told my mother.

My mother got very upset when she heard this and was screaming and shouting. My sister Despo took the blame for me and said that it was her. She was my sister and wanted to cover for me. Then my mother started shouting at her and she ran away and slept the night somewhere in a sleeping bag. It was a mess.

My mother was just trying to protect us but she was threatening to tell my father about it all and I was really frightened. I don't know why I did it, other than that I was scared, but I took about ten Extra-Panadol tablets because I couldn't face things.

Absolutely nothing happened – they had no effect whatsoever and afterwards I realised how stupid I had been.

On 18 October 1981 it was the birthday of Christakis so I saved up my money to buy him his first present from me which was a silver chain which I had his name written on."

***

The Greek word for engagement is *'arrabhon'* or *'aravonas'* and is derived from the Hebrew word *'erabon'* which translates as a pledge or guarantee.

(Andry):

"My father put a notice in the *'Phileleftheros'* newspaper on the 1 November 1981 to announce that I was officially engaged to Christakis.

A few days before the official announcement the inevitable happened in his car in an empty field just outside Limassol. We had completed our relationship. I must admit that it wasn't what I thought it would be plus it was painful and uncomfortable.

Prior to this his father came to our house to ask my father if he would agree to us getting engaged. My father asked where Chris was, as it was the normal custom for him to be there, but for some reason he just didn't come.

This type of meeting used to be called a *'broksenya'* or *'dunurcu'* where dowry's used to be discussed, and the bride's family used to have to commit to providing land, a house or a large deposit to buy one.

As we were a poor family there was no chance of us providing a dowry!

***

Chris's father was named Michalis, but everyone called him *'Michalos'* because he was so fat.

His family lived in Asomotas village which sits partly in the Akrotiri Sovereign Bases area. Before the invasion there were some Turkish Cypriots living there but they left. The name of the village comes from the word *'Asomati',* which is a word used for the two Archangels Michael and Gabriele, which means *'without body'.*

His family were refugees and originally came from Ayios Sergios, a very big village near to Famagusta, which had a population of some two thousand before the invasion and occupation.

Most of those living in the village were originally Greek Cypriots with just a very small number of Turkish Cypriots who left in the late 1950s. Afterwards it was re-populated solely by Turkish Cypriots, some of whom were the original occupants, as well as Turkish settlers from the mainland.

I know that when Christakis was just seven years of age he worked in a factory opposite his home where they made haloumi cheese. He was paid in cheese for his efforts.

There is a church in the village called Ayios Sergios and Vanchos which has a story attached to it to the effect that whilst a man was in his coffin during his funeral he suddenly became alive and sat up.

Christakis also worked in fields, digging up potatoes, at the age of fourteen in Xylophago, where they lived for a while as refugees. They were called the red fields because the soil was coloured red. Later on they moved to Asomatos in Limassol.

At some stage, before it was all official, my mother was chatting to a neighbour, and one of her sisters, who said that she knew Michalos because his girlfriend was living next to her in the second refugee settlement in Trachoni. My mother was surprised and shocked at this announcement as he was quite big and she didn't think he was capable of this.

He looked like the figure of a *'Bhudda'* and she expressed this view openly.

Someone obviously told Michalos what she had said because he came around the house shouting and threatening to call the engagement off. My mother responded, *"I haven't said anything - I just said what I saw and if you want to do so then do it!!"*

This was something that never happened because we didn't let it.

My future father-in-law never divorced. He had four children with his girlfriend, and rumours of another one with another woman. With his wife he had thirteen children that lived and I believe that they also lost some.

My relationship with my father-in-law was not brilliant as many times he tried to interfere between me and Christakis. It was his nature to try always to get involved in his children's lives and to influence them to the best of his opinion.

I was young, and very stubborn, and I never accepted my elder's opinions or advice. I had my own understanding for life and I was following it strictly.

On the other hand my mother-in-law was a *'golden'* lady that suffered a lot in her life trying to support all her family with love and affection.

I remember once being out in a small forest in Asomatos with her, taking out the sheep from their fold to eat grass when she said to me, 'When I die don't cry for me as I will be rest in peace.' She was so kind that whatever you asked her she wouldn't say no, no matter how tired she was or how many jobs she had to do. She was one of a kind!

***

The priest in my village was named Papa Evagelos but was also known as Papas Skouloukos, which translates to the name *'worm'*. He is dead now but was a bit of a character and was a regular in the coffee shops in Trachoni. One day his wife *'papadia'* was looking for him and she stood outside a coffee shop shouting for him to come out. He was a bit afraid of her and eventually did as he was told – he couldn't escape from her!

The priest subsequently came to our house in Trachoni to bless us both. My parents, my sisters and brother were there, together with his father and mother, and a younger sister. We invited other members of his family but they didn't come.

I didn't have that many clothes so I wore my school uniform, a black skirt and white blouse.

We put long tables out on the veranda at the front of the house to eat, but there were quite a few empty chairs.

I remember at my engagement party we played an old tape that my father had. I think that he bought an AKAI cine-recorder from Germany and he played old songs of Tolis Voskopoulos, and Yiannis Poulopoulos, who were very popular singers at the time.

Tolis Voskopoulos was born in Greece in 1940 and was a legend of Greek music as well as starring in films and appearing in the theatre in hits such as *'Dream Lovers'*. One of my favourite songs of his was *'One woman, one love, one life'*.

Yiannis Poulopoulos had lots of hit songs in the 1960s/70s/ and 80s and sold the fourth highest number of albums of all Greek singers. By 1966 his records sold widely and many of his songs featured in films.

On another tape, which I think was recorded at Maro's engagement, my mother was singing her favourite song which went,

'Keramidi, keramidi, eftiaksa ena kalivi to' eftiaksa me

chilious kopous

tin agapi mou na valo

pio politimo sto kosmo

apo aftin den echo allo'

This translates to,

'Brick by brick I build a home,

I build it with so much effort,

to place my love,

I have nothing more precious than her, in this world.'

I guess it was a song that touched the heart of my mother and reflected her wishes in life and I always remember her singing it.

She had another song that she loved very much which went, *'Asta ta mallakia sou, anakatomena, Asta na' nemizoune stin trelli notia.....'*

This translates to *'Leave your hair loose, leave them blow against the crazy wind.....'*

My father was also someone who had very deep feelings and he used to regularly *'chant'* hymns and prayers in the churches in Trachoni and at Agias Napa in Limassol.

We used to enjoy listening to the tapes but one day my grandmother Irinou got all upset as we were listening to one, and grabbed the tape from the machine and tore it in pieces!

***

After the engagement, as is the custom, Christakis moved to our house and we had our own room. I was sixteen at the time. There were only two bedrooms; we had one whilst my parents had the other, and we had to put beds into the living room for my sister Despo and my brother Michalis.

Christakis was working as a builder and I carried on at school. Almost every night he used to spend his time in the 'coffee-shop' with his friends and would normally come back after 10pm. It caused a lot of arguments between us.

During one argument when I got cross with him Christakis hit me and we split for a while because of it. We got back together because we loved each other and he said that he wouldn't do it again.

Domestic violence in Cyprus is quite common. Within the family my elder sister was abused, as well as my youngest sister. There is very little official support for women who find themselves in such situations, and generally speaking women are placed under a lot of pressure from their families to stay with the husband, especially if there are any children involved.

The victim in such cases almost always comes second and often gets very little sympathy.

Whilst we were engaged we went to Nicosia General Hospital for some blood tests to see if we were carrying the *'Mediterranean stigma'* as we had to have a paper to allow us to get a marriage licence. They advised couples who both had it not to get married as they stood a high risk of having sick children.

I have never been good with needles and a nurse tried several times to take some blood. When she eventually got the needle in I fainted and they just managed to catch me.

When the results came it turned out that I was a carrier but Christakis was not so we were okay.

Socially we used to go out with one of his best friends Kakos and his fiancée Ritsa. We used to go out a lot together and sometimes we would go into Limassol and have a meze in a tavern, and go to wedding parties too, as they had common friends coming from the same village.

We also used to go out with another couple - Stephanos was a friend of Christakis and Andry was a schoolmate. We used to go to the beach together and sometimes go for a drive to Paphos, or just generally spend time together."

***

Meze is short for *'mezedhes'* and means *'small bits'*. It can include up to thirty dishes would can consist of either a meat meze, or fish meze, or a mixture of both. A traditional meze can include the following:

Black or green olives with dips with Pitta Bread and a Village Salad,

Snails in tomato sauce,

Pickled capers and cauliflower,

Carrots sliced and in vinegar,

Sardines or tiny red mullet,

Calamari,

Halloumi Cheese - fried,

Cyprus Ham – called Lounza

Meatballs in a tomato sauce,

Pork Chops

Smoked Cyprus Sausages

Beef Afelia,

Moussaka, cooked in small round dishes,

Stifado,

Pork Kebab Souvlakia,

Kleftiko baked in a sealed oven, Chicken from the grill,

Fried potatoes,

Fried tomatoes with eggs, Keftedes

Koupepia

Lamb chops

Choriatika makaronia with angri (pasta)

Kapary in vinegar,

Agrelia with beaten eggs,

Tzaniki, tahini, taramosalata dips,

Fried courgettes with beaten eggs,

Fried tomatoes with eggs,

Fresh fruit or fruit in syrup,

Mpaklava a sticky sweet with honey in it

***

(Andry):

"In the fifth year at school my friend Lydia Pelopida remembers that we held the *'Miss Enato'* competition which some of the boys thought was going to be like a competition to find the most beautiful girl, and maybe they thought that we were going to show some flesh if we wore swimming costumes. We turned it into a hilarious joke and did the opposite.

My friend Lydia won the title but joked that it meant that she had won the title for being the ugliest girl in the class!"

Actually Lydia is a very beautiful woman.

Figure 85 Trachoni – Lina's 3rd birthday party – Andry at rear

(1981)

Figure 86 Green Monday – Andry far left (1981)

Figure 87 Trachoni - Andry and Anthoulla (1981)

Figure 88 Trachoni – Andry's father/Michalis on the bike of her

former husband Christakis (1981)

Figure 89 Bus overturned in a dam near to Moniatis Village

(13.3.1981) Cyprus Mail

Figure 90 Bus overturned in a dam near to Moniatis Village

Figure 91 Green Monday (circa 1981) – Andry rear second from

right

Chapter Eighteen

1982

An Unexpected Pregnancy

(Andry):

"I started taking the pill when we began sleeping together. I didn't like it but I didn't think that I had any other options as I didn't want to become pregnant at that point.

After a while I stopped taking it because I started to put weight on.

Christakis agreed with me that I should to go to the doctors to have the coil fitted but whilst I was waiting he spoke to his eldest sister who advised him not to let me have it. She told him that if I used it I might not be able to have children and put a question in his head about what he would do with me if I couldn't have children!

Christakis came and told me what his sister had said and told me that I couldn't have the coil. He was influenced by her, and there was no point arguing with him - I had to do as I was told even that I was not happy at all.

***

Christakis as a refugee, and me as a member of a big family, were entitled to a fund to build a house on our own land, or in one of the refugee settlements.

As we had been living in Trachoni for some years, and we were engaged, I was allowed to have a piece of land to build on.

After I received my piece of land we started looking to create some plans for our home. I wanted a one-storey house with no stairs, thinking in advance that stairs would be dangerous for future children. My father took us to an architect to explain how we wanted our house to be and after telling him what we wanted he came up with two draft plans.

The first one was a very big lounge with stairs leading to the bedrooms, a master bedroom with a bathroom, a second bathroom and two other bedrooms, a big kitchen, living room, a study room and a shower room with a toilet for guests.

It was huge plus with the stairs I didn't like it so we went for the second plan.

As Christakis was a builder he marked the foundations and started to dig the designated area. The stony ground was too hard to break by hand and we ended up bringing a big digger with a diamond head on it to do the job.

The iron was ordered and we had to prepare the iron columns. In Cyprus buildings are constructed with concrete foundations and pillars to withstand earthquakes. I remember that a carob tree by the next housing plot was the ideal place to do the preparations under the shade.

I learnt to do it as well so I was helping at every opportunity. I was not scared to get my hands dirty and to work hard. We couldn't afford to pay people to do it anyway.

At the same time we applied to the government help. It was a very slow procedure and took months to complete the necessary forms, as we had to provide all sorts of documents.

Eventually we were informed that the money had been approved although it was only about five thousand pounds, and then they took some of that from us because we had already done the foundations. We were not lucky with this project.

The house took us years to finish as we didn't have the money and it was actually a few days before Christmas 1987 before we finally moved in."

***

(Andry):

"In the same year, in May, another tragic death occurred in the village. A family who lived nearby were called Panaretos. They had a son Demetris who was just seventeen at the time. Because he was older than me I wasn't really mixing with him but his brother Marios, was in my class, and Loulla his sister was in the same school.

Demetris got sick quite suddenly with leukaemia and then after a few months he died. There was a big funeral in the village. It is quite normal for families to become very emotional at funerals and to let their feelings come out with people wailing and crying out, especially when it is someone who dies so young.

After a death it is traditional for the families to attend memorials for them in church and to take *'kolifa'*, which are made from wheat, to share with people there and to wish *'God rest his soul'*.

The memorials start after three days, six days and nine days. Then they go to three weeks and forty days, and finally three months, six months, nine months and twelve months. Thereafter the memorial is an annual service. There is also one day every year to remember those that die naturally, and another day for those people that die after an accident. Prayers are said and a priest reads out the name of the dead person, following which there is a small ceremony at the graveside.

There was a small cemetery in the Old Village, which is where Demetris was buried. When the new church was finished another larger cemetery was created nearby.

The practice is to have a marble cross marking the person's grave which bears the name of the person and the dates when born and died. In recent times it has also become practice to place a picture of the deceased in the centre of the cross.

I used to go to church almost every Sunday at about 8am until I was a teenager and then I started not to go so regularly. I am a believer but I wouldn't say that I am very close to the church.

***

One day, whilst we were still engaged, we went to visit some of the relatives of Christakis in Larnaca. I was on the back of his motorbike and we were on a straight road. We had just overtaken a car at maybe 100 kph when suddenly the rear tyre on his bike exploded.

The bike started zig-zagging across the road from one side to another before Christakis managed to stop. We were lucky not to have been killed as there were cars on the road. Christakis burst into tears and I was in shock. We walked to Kofinou and found a garage. They took us back to the bike and got it fixed before we carried on.

***

At some point I became pregnant by mistake. I thought at first that it was just a delay in my period and I spoke to my sister-in-law about this. She told to me to take some pills from a pharmacy for the period to come. The pharmacist said to me though that if I was pregnant and took them then I would have to have an abortion.

It was Christmas 1982 and it was confirmed that I was pregnant. I was still at school – it sounds hard but I couldn't have a baby as they would have stopped me from completing my education and taking my exams. I just couldn't be pregnant and engaged at school. It just wasn't allowed.

I was very upset with everything that happened - firstly because of the involvement of his sister and then for getting pregnant. I was very young to know what the right thing to do was and I felt that I wasn't getting the right advice."

Figure 92 Trachoni - Andry's birthday (circa 1982)

Figure 93 Trachoni – Andry on her scooter (1982)

Chapter Nineteen

1983

The Marriage

Although the family was facing yet another challenge, New Year's Day was celebrated in the usual traditional Cypriot fashion.

(Andry):

"As usual New Year was started by eating a cake which was baked on New Year's Eve by my mother. The minute that midnight passed we cut the cake.

The cake was cut by my father, and the first piece was for Jesus, the second for Santa Maria, and then the third piece for Ayios Vasilis, then him, then my mother, followed by us, the children.

Ayios Vasilis, unlike his western counterpart, was a tall thin man with a black beard and piercing eyes, but he was kind and thoughtful and helped the poor whilst he was the Bishop of Caesarea. He died on January 1st 379 AD, which is why he is celebrated on this day and why children have come to expect presents or *'gifts'*.

A silver coin is placed inside the cake, wrapped in silver-foil, and whoever finds it will considered to be the luckiest member of the family for that year. On the top would be placed almond nuts in the shape of *'Happy New Year'* and the year in numbers, known as the *'Vasilopitta'*. If the coin is found in the first three pieces it is kept for the house. If it is found by an individual they keep it with them for good luck.

The cake is part of the celebrations relating to *'Ayios Vasilis'*, who is the Patron Saint of the New Year. They used to sing a song called *'Ayios Vasilis – the person who is going to bring the presents.'*

On 6th January we celebrate *'Epifania'* when it is also traditional to make *'loukoumades'* which are one of the oldest recorded desserts in the world. In ancient Greece the dough balls, which are fried and soaked in honey, were served to the winners of the Olympic Games.

We also had a tradition of throwing the *'loukoumades'* onto the roofs of our houses so that the *'evil creatures'*, the *'kalikaztsaroi'* would eat them and go away. We also used to throw sausages onto the roof for the same reason - actually it was also good for the birds!

Whilst we were throwing these things onto the roof we would sing a song,

'Titsin Titsin Loukaniko komati kserotiano na fan i kalikantzari Na fasin ke na fiousin'

Basically the song was about telling the creatures to eat and go away!!

***

(Andry):

"I had an abortion in a private hospital in January 1983, although the doctor nearly said no to carrying one out. I was put to sleep for the operation and I was home again within the same day. At the time I didn't think about it too much but over the years I have thought about it a lot, and it is a painful memory.

I wondered so many times whether I had done the right thing. Because of the pills there was a risk that the baby would not be born normally.

In our religion it is a sin to have an abortion and my mind was everywhere trying to make the right decision.

***

In the same year my sister Chrystalla gave birth to her son Constantinos on the 21 April.

As the newborn baby he took all of our attention and love. I remember that I used to visit every day to spend time with him.

***

We were thirty-four girls in the class, in our final year, and another friend Lydia Pelopida recalls an incident when another *'pretend fight'* took place in a mathematics lesson, involving two other girls Flora and Tonia. The teacher just didn't know what to do and the class was in chaos.

In that final year seven girls in my class were formally engaged. My teacher knew about this and boasted that he would be able to easily say which of the girls were. He correctly guessed six of the girls but couldn't get the seventh right. When my friends told him that it was me he acted surprised and said that he thought that I would have had more sense.

My school-friend Andry Ioannou remembers that after she did her final examinations for history the teacher asked her what mark he thought he should give. She replied that no-one was perfect and on that basis she would be happy with eighteen from twenty. He looked at her and said that because she had been so humble he would give her twenty from twenty.

Andry was very quiet at school and loved looking at the birds and the butterflies. She also hated doing PE so when we were running round and round the school she used to find somewhere to hide and then join in at the end!

I finished school in about May or June and said goodbye to many of my classmates. There were many different characters. One of the students was considered to be one of the brightest in the class. That was until she was caught cheating and found with a piece of paper with the answers written on during a test!

Throughout my years at Gymnasium and Lyceum schools I was getting an extra diploma for finishing with distinction. I was always a good student and never had any absences from school. For all of the years I was a member of the class committee with different roles, as well as being a member of the school choir, and playing the guitar. I took part in school theatres and events, and was interested for everything that was going on. They were happy years for me.

***

Straight after school I went to work in an offshore company in Limassol doing a secretarial job. I worked with a Scottish girl called Diane who was a year older than me and was from Aberdeen.

I think that she was in Cyprus with her mother and sister and we got on really well.

In about August 1983 I stopped taking any precautions as I wanted to get pregnant, knowing that I was going to be married in October and didn't mind if I was already a couple of months.

Nothing happened and every time I had a period I was shouting and screaming - I just wanted to have a baby then. I know that to some people this will not sound logical given my experience earlier in the year but logic did not apply.

I wasn't pregnant when I got married but it was not unusual in those days for this to happen. As long as the couple were engaged it was accepted.

To some extent this is the culture that remains today. It is not acceptable in the eyes of most families for a couple to have casual sex but if they get formally engaged the boy moves into the girl's home and because the relationship is official it is okay for them to sleep together.

In those years the engagement was official and covered by law whereas now it is not."

***

Up to one hundred years ago, some weddings in Cyprus were arranged by matchmakers known as *'Proxenitra',* who were usually women.

They avoided leap-years, which were deemed to be unlucky, and common phrases included, *'I ora kali'* which translates to *'May the wedding day be good'* or *'Kala stephana'* which means *'Good wedding crowns'*.

(Andry):

"We were married in the Greek Orthodox Church, Agios Mamas in Trachoni, on the 9 October 1983 – I was a month off being eighteen years of age.

Before the wedding we took the wedding invitations around to family, and friends, and people that our families knew. It was, and still is, not unusual for hundreds of people to attend a wedding, indeed it can be whole villages. In some cases where rich or influential people see their children getting married, thousands can turn up – and all of them are fed and entertained.

My wedding dress was made by Roulla and we bought the material from Pafitis Store in Limassol. It cost fifty Cyprus Pounds, which was a lot of money, but to buy a dress would have cost a lot more.

The best-man *'koumbaros'* was also named Christakis – *'Takis'* for short.

My chief bridesmaid *'koumbara'* was my school-friend Anthoulla, who I have known from the age of six years, and also lived in Trachoni.

I had four bridesmaids, Lisa, Loukia, and Lina on my side, as well as Loukia his sister, and Sami as a pageboy who wore blue and white.

My dress was white, it was long, with a veil, and I wore short white gloves.

Before we went to the church we did a ceremony at the house just before we left. It is supposed to celebrate virginity for the bride but often it's a tradition rather than a fact!

Musicians played the violin *'laouto'* and sang whilst my parents, my chief bridesmaid, and close friends wrapped a red scarf around my waist and head three times, and blessed me with the fumes of olive leaves and lavender.

At the house of my husband-to-be they carried out what's called the *'last shave'* with family and friends present, whilst his best man shaved him before he got dressed.

Christakis wore a white suit with a waistcoat and a red cravat and the best man wore exactly the same.

They also placed the red scarf around him in the same way to wish for fertility and virility whilst musicians sang and played traditional songs such as *'Ora Kali'*.

They drove me to the church in Trachoni Village with my mother and father, and Anthoulla. It was in one of Christakis's elder-brother's cars – a brand new Daihatsu Charmant.

As is the custom Christakis met me at the church door with flowers and my parents officially gave me away to him.

As we met outside the church the priest placed us opposite each other and with a loud voice said to Christakis, "Christakis you like to be married to Androulla? This is your last chance to change your mind and go away."

Everyone was laughing with his announcement and Christakis shouted back, "Yes I do want to marry her of course!"

He walked towards me, gave me the flowers and kissed me. The guests asked him to kiss me again and the photographer was kept busy.

We walked down the aisle together with both sets of parents following behind. It is traditional for the parents to remain standing with the couple throughout the whole of the service. The priest was Papa Neophitos and known with the nickname *'Papa Skouloukos'*.

During the service bread *'prosfora'* was given to us by the priest and red Cypriot wine *'koumandaria'* to drink, symbolizing the wedding at Cana in Galilee, where Christ blessed the marriage and converted water into wine.

We did the ceremony of the wedding crowns *'stefana'* where the priest placed a ceremonial headband on my head, symbolizing god's blessings, and a similar crown on Christakis's head.

The priest said a prayer and then tied them together.

The marriage crowns are extremely important to the couple – they are saved, or placed on display, and you may even be buried in them – the ribbon that binds them together representing the lasting union that has to be kept intact for a lifetime.

Wearing the *'stefana'* we exchanged wedding rings, with our names inside, on the fourth finger of each right hand to recognise that *'God's right hand is the hand that blesses'*.

Then we performed the *'Dance of Isaiah'* with the priest leading us three times around the table that held the Gospel and the Cross. The best-man and chief bridesmaid followed us round behind holding the *'stefana'* in place. We drank from the common cup three times followed by a reading of the Epistle and the Gospel.

It is the custom whilst the couple go around the table for the *'head koumparos'* to protect the groom from the rest of the *'koumparos'* as they try to give the groom a *'strong smack'* on the back. The *'head koumparos'* is receiving them all. That is the custom.

The priest blessed us, removed the *'stefana'* and asked God to grant us a long, and happy life together.

At some point during the service the custom is for the priest to say, *'women shall fear her husband'*. At this point the first one, bride or groom, to put their foot on top of the others will run the house. We agreed however from before the service that neither of us would do this.

Finally the priest separated our joined hands, which was to show that only God could separate us from one another.

At this point the parents, and the very close family, come forward to congratulate the couple and to kiss the *'stefana'*.

If any of them were divorced they were not allowed to kiss the *'stefana'* as it was considered to be bad luck.

The ceremony lasted about forty-five minutes, to one hour, and throughout there were religious chants from the priest – *'the God, the Son, the Holy Spirit'*.

During the ceremony the practice is for friends and relatives to write down their names as *'koumparos'* and *'koumera'*, which means they witness the wedding. Along with this they then give a fixed amount of money. I don't remember how much they each gave for our wedding but I think it was between five and ten pounds.

We gave sugared almonds *'koufetta'* to guests as they left the church, with each small bag containing an odd number of almonds, which could not be divided up equally. They are meant to represent unity and their egg-shape represents fertility. The firm texture symbolizes the endurance of an everlasting marriage, and the white coating purity, and the sweetness of a new life.

The *'koufetta'* is normally taken by young girls and placed under their pillows, before being eaten, in order for them to dream about the man that they will marry.

As we left the church guests threw rice at us.

We did the *'congratulations'* outside the church, although mostly people stand in a greeting line at the reception, which is known as the *'Hairetisis'*.

It is customary for people to give money in envelopes known as *'fakelaki'*, which are put into a box. The idea is to help with a house deposit and I think that we finished up with about one thousand Cyprus Pounds and lots of small presents, glasses and things for our future house.

After the *'Hairetisis'* we went to Kollosi Castle for some photographs.

We used to visit the place when I was at school. It is a former Crusader stronghold and is very near to Kollosi village. A castle was originally built on the site by the Franks, and then the present one was built in 1454 in the same place by the Commander of Kollosi Louise de Magnac.

The length of each of the square walls outside is 16 meters whereas the inside measures 13.5 meters. Because it was built with such strong walls it has withstood earthquakes in the area.

We also went for more photographs to the Municipal Park in Limassol.

After this we went to a taverna in Limassol that did receptions. It doesn't exist anymore - there were about one hundred people there, and our families contributed towards the preparation of the food.

At this point I changed from my wedding dress into a black shiny dress, which was long, just over the knees, and with a long cut at the back, down to the waist. My sister Roulla designed it and made it especially for me.

The guests at the reception had *'kleftiko'* with potatoes, salad, chicken and pastitio, which is a baked pasta dish that contains mince pork.

We had some sort of disco with a *'DJ'*. Normally at weddings people dance the *'Tsifteteli'* – a simple form of belly-dance, which men and women do separately, or in pairs, and *'Zeibekkiko'*, a dance which a single individual performs to the synchronised clapping of a circle of people, whilst musicians played the *'bouzouki'*.

It is also customary to pin money onto the newlyweds during a dance which is called *'choros tou androjinou'* but we didn't do this.

I tossed my bouquet at the end of the evening to the single girls – the one to catch it was to be the next to marry, and we went back home at about 1am. We had no honeymoon as we wanted to save the money to build our house.

There are other traditions surrounding weddings. One of the ones that we didn't do before, or at our wedding, was the *'Krevati'* dance, where they use a mattress. First they toss rice and a young boy, or girl, in it. The tradition is to do with fertility and for hoping that the first- born will be a male child.

There is a feeling that male children will be less of a burden than girls and also of course they will carry the family name on which is really important, whereas the girls take their husbands surname This causes a lot of stress in families and certainly did in ours until Michalis, my brother, came along.

My friend Diane came to our wedding but afterwards I left the job and went to work somewhere else. I saw Diane at some point after the wedding and she told me that her sister had been killed in a car accident on the highway. Her boyfriend, who was driving, lived. I think speeding was involved which unfortunately is not an unusual occurrence in Cyprus. I lost touch with her after that."

***

On the 15 November 1983 Rauf Denktash declared the occupied parts of northern Cyprus as the *'Turkish Republic of Northern Cyprus'* in an effort to create an independent state. To this day only Turkey recognises this position.

***

(Andry):

"After we got married we lived with my mother.

Roulla lived above us, and every morning her daughter Lina, who was still only two years of age, used to come downstairs to our room to see Christakis – she really loved him and said that she was going to marry him when she was older!

***

One of the restaurants that we used to visit quite regularly on a Saturday night, after we got married, was called *'Antonaros'* in Limassol. There was no music but it was a very popular place with lots of pictures on the walls, sayings in Greek, and photos of singers and well-known people who had visited the place.

One of the sayings that I will never forget was, *'Did my wife say have two drinks and be home by eleven, or did she say to have eleven drinks and be home by two?'*

Figure 94 Andry finishing school (1983)

Figure 95 Andry finishing school (1983)

Figure 96 The class of 6th grade Lycium – Ayios Antonis,

Limassol – Andry front row far right (1983)

Figure 97 Trachoni - The birthday of Andry's former husband

Christakis (1983)

Figure 98 Andry's father Costas on her first wedding day (1983)

Figure 99 The wedding of Andry Christou to Christakis

Christou 9 October 1983

Epilogue

(Andry):

"After my father finally left home my mother started working in one of the *'Sun Island Packing Houses'*, which made juices and fruits in syrup.

My mother finally divorced my father on the 2 October 1992 when I was pregnant with my daughter Loukia. We passed from the registry offices in Limassol and got the divorce papers and next day I gave birth to Loukia which was the fourth of my miracles - I now had my complete family.

***

In June 1992 another miracle occurred, the story of which is very familiar to me, and one which I would describe as follows:

Eleni Leonida Skourou came from Limassol where she lived with her husband Leonidas. At the time she was forty-seven years of age and was facing serious health problems with only 15% of her heart working properly. Her doctor informed her that she needed an operation urgently to save her life, and her husband asked God for his help.

At 5.30am on the morning that her operation was due Leonidas was visited by Saint George, and Saint Andrew, who spoke to him about the Church of St George, a deserted monastery in Happy Valley, in the Sovereign Bases Area.

From that day Eleni was cured of her heart condition, and after being re-examined by her doctor all of her medication, some thirteen tablets a day, was stopped.

The couple subsequently found the abandoned monastery and in a cave nearby they found an icon of Saint George the Great Martyr.

A spring of fresh water comes out from the ground in the cave and people refer to it as *'agiasma'* (holy water) and drink from it in the belief that it will cure them from illness.

In Byzantine times the Bishops of Cyprus used to hold council meetings at the location and they were referred to as the *'Council of the Land'* – *'Symvouli tou Kyriou'*.

A year after the discovery they started the restoration of the church and devoted their lives to it.

The restored church is now called *'Church of St George of Symvoulas'*.

It is a place I have visited many times where you can find peace listening to the sound of the breeze amongst the trees, which surround it, and have time to reflect."

***

(Andry):

"Having lived in different parts of Cyprus during my childhood I can say that Cypriots have a lot of fun talking about each other.

They have long-standing views on each other which in some ways could be deemed as rather humorous but sometimes is a bit more serious!

People who live in Limassol will often comment that the men from Nicosia are *'Children of their mothers'* – meaning that *'the men are under their mothers skirts'*. They resent the fact that Nicosia is seen as the place of central authority for Cyprus.

Those from Nicosia will say quite simply that Limassol is a *'Fuck Town'* meaning that it is always lively night and day.

Residents from Larnaca are often referred to as *'Gypsies'*, whilst if you come from Paphos other Cypriots make comments about the different dialect that they speak.

There is one thing for sure and that is that we always have something, and someone, to talk about!

***

I passed my driving test when I was eighteen years old and drove Christakis's car although I also had a bike.

Driving in Cyprus is an, 'interesting' experience and you have to be prepared for the expected and the unexpected!

Wherever we drive we always try to park the closest to the place we are visiting so if it's a shop we want to try to park outside the front door. The problem is that so does everyone else! We didn't have mobile phones in those days but my husband now routinely jokes that Cypriots need four hands to drive – one for the steering wheel, one for a cigarette, one for the mobile phone, and one to hang out of the window to catch the breeze!

This is a bit of an exaggeration but you do see all of these things happening.

***

We may be a small nation but we are steeped in history, and our culture, traditions, and religion make us feel rich and fulfilled.

We do not lead perfect lives but then who does!
Above all else through hard times we remain full of hope for the futures of our children. As the Christou family were created so the next generations followed.

My children, and their cousins, are now building the next one......."

(Andry Christou-Layton and Michael Layton – May 2017)

Figure 100 Andry with her mother Loukia and a picture of her

mother's wedding day (2017)

Figure 101 Andry with her four children –

Andry/Valentinos/Lenos/Marios/Loukia (2011)

Figure 102 Andry with her brother and sisters

Michalis/Despo/Andry/Chrystalla/Roulla/Maro (2007)

Figure 103 Andry with her father Costas (May 2016)

Figure 104 Andry with her granddaughter Christina (May 2016)

Figure 105 Andry with her mother Loukia (May 2016)

Figure 106 Andry with Christina and husband and co-author

Michael Layton (May 2016)

Schedule of Photographs

(Unless otherwise stated the source of the material rests with the co-authors)

Fig 1) The Cyprus Flag

Fig 2) Map of Cyprus

Fig 3) Map of Cyprus

Fig 4) Loukia - Andry's mother before her marriage. (Pre-1956)

Fig 5) Group picture - the wedding of Andry's parents in August 1956

Fig 6) Andry's parents – Costas & Loukia on the day of their wedding in August 1956

Fig 7) Loukia - Andry's mother (Post 1956)

Fig 8) Costas - Andry's father (Post 1956)

Fig 9) Antigoni & Christodoulos - the parents of Andry's mother in later life

Fig 10) Irinou - the mother of Andry's father in later life

Fig 11) Aristotelis - the brother of Andry's mother in his 30s/40s

Fig 12) Agios Paraskevi Church in Geroskipou, Paphos

Fig 13) Agios Paraskevi Church in Geroskipou, Paphos

Fig 14) Andry on a rocking horse (circa 1967)

Fig 15) Andry (centre) with sisters – Chrystalla/Maro/Roulla (circa 1967)

Fig 16) Andry (circa 1967)

Fig 17) Famagusta (Varosia) before 1974

Fig 18) Andry – front centre – Koulis and Christakis to the right at back – 1968

Fig 19) At Agios Nicolaos – Chrystalla/Andry/Christodoulos/Despo (circa 1969/70)

Fig 20) At Agios Nicolaos – Despo/Andry/Chrystalla (circa 1969/70)

Fig 21) Paphos area – Andry's parents (circa 1969/70)

Fig 22) At Agios Nicolaos – Andry's mother with Christodoulos (circa 1970)

Fig 23) At Agios Nicolaos – The birthday of Roulla – Maro/Despo/Andry's mother/Roulla/A friend Garifallo (which means 'carnation' in English) Andry/Chrystalla (circa 1970)

Fig 24) Amanda - Andry's friend (circa 1971)

Fig 25) Julie - Andry's friend (circa 1971)

Fig 26) Kyrenia – Andry's father/His Aunt Theodora and her husband. (circa 1971)

Fig 27) Kyrenia – A family gathering - Andry front row far right (circa 1971)

Fig 28) Famagusta – Antigoni & family gathering - Andry in middle of front row - (circa1971)

Fig 29) Agios Nicolaos – Chrystalla/Amanda holding a pigeon/Andry (circa 1971)

Fig 30) Outside the kiosk at Limassol – Andry on right (circa 1971)

Fig 31) Fighting Birds

Fig 32) 2nd grade Elementary School Trachoni Class Photo – Andry middle row 3rd from left (circa 1972/3)

Fig 33) The old 'Agios Mamas' church in Trachoni Village

Fig 34) The new 'Agios Mamas' church in Trachoni Village

Fig 35) Coffee shop in Trachoni once run by Costas Christou

Fig 36) 'Constantinos & Evripidis' – picture in Trachoni Coffee Shop

Fig 37) Kyrenia before 1974

Fig 38) 1st Grade Elementary School Trachoni Class Photo – Andry front row second from right – 1971/1972

Fig 39) Agios Athanasios – Roulla/Maro/Chrystalla/Despo/Andry – front row on right (circa 1973)

Fig 40) Trachoni – Roulla/Despo/Andry/Chrystalla (circa 1973)

Fig 41) 2nd Grade Elementary School Trachoni Class Photo – Andry front row second from left - 1972/1973

Fig 42) Rock of Aphrodite – Paphos – Michalis/Maro (circa 1974)

Fig 43) Rock of Aphrodite – Paphos – Roulla (circa 1974)

Fig 44) Trachoni – Michalis/Andry on pedal cycle/Chrystalla/Despo/Roulla (circa 1974)

Fig 45) Limassol Old Port – Andry's father Costas/Michalis/Andry's mother Loukia (circa 1974)

Fig 46) Andry's father Costas as a volunteer soldier (circa 1974)

Fig 47) Andry's father Costas as a volunteer soldier with a Greek officer (circa 1974)

Fig 48) Picture of the certificate for bravery awarded to Andry's father for his actions in 1974

Fig 49) Tasos Charalambous – 1974

Fig 50) Chrystalla/Roulla/Despo/Loukia – mother/Michalis/Maro/Andry seated (circa 1974)

Fig 51) Wedding of Kokos and Maro (5 May 1974) – Andry sat in front

Fig 52) 3rd Grade Elementary School Trachoni Class Photo – Andry far left middle row – 1973/1974

Fig 53) A road-block at Avdimou – Malcolm Halliday on far right (July 1974) (Ack - MH)

Fig 54) The aftermath of a demonstration at RAF Akrotiri – (1974) (Ack - MH)

Fig 55) David Woolmer RAF (circa 1974) in Cyprus (Ack - DW)

Fig 56) An original note left at David Woolmer's address in Platres, Cyprus following the invasion in 1974 (Ack - DW)

Fig 57) Nr. Nicosia – Andry's grandfather Christos 'Mavris' & Andry's mother Loukia (circa 1975)

Fig 58) Nr. Nicosia – Andry's grandfather Christos 'Mavris' & Andry's father Costas (circa 1975)

Fig 59) Nr. Nicosia – Family gathering – Andry front row (circa 1975)

Fig 60) Agios Athanasios – Andry (circa 1975)

Fig 61) Trachoni – Andry's father Costas with his new car (circa 1975)

Fig 62) Trachoni – 4th grade Elementary Class – Andry middle row far left (12.4.1975)

Fig 63) Schools Competitions – Andry front row far left – wearing no. 3 for Trachoni village (1977)

Fig 64) Competition between schools – Andry far left (1977)

Fig 65) Competition between schools – Andry front row far left (1977)

Fig 66) Lania Village - S.K. EDEK talk by Vasos Lissarides – Andry seated front row 2nd left facing the speaker (circa 1977)

Fig 67) Limassol – Palestinian children visiting (1977)

Fig 68) Limassol Harbour – on Sami's yacht – Andry front left (1977)

Fig 69) Paphos Port by the castle – Andry far right holding a swordfish (1977)

Fig 70) Sami/Roulla/Andrys mother/Michalis/Chrystalla/Despo/Andry – with Aphrodite's Rock in the background (1977)

Fig 71) School-friend Christos in centre of picture – Andry to the right holding nephew Kostas (circa 1977)

Fig 72) 6th Grade Elementary School Trachoni Class Photo – Andry middle row second right - 1976/1977

Fig 73) Governors Beach – Andry far left (1978)

Fig 74) Governors Beach – Costas/Andry/Despo/Chrystalla (1978)

Fig 75) Trachoni – Despo/Andry holding her niece Lina/Michalis (1979)

Fig 76) Troodos – family gathering – Andry far left at rear (circa 1979)

Fig 77) Troodos – family gathering – Andry far left at rear (circa 1979)

Fig 78) Picture of Andry in her *'best wishes'* book (2.3.1979)

Fig 79) Curium Amphitheatre – Andry (1980)

Fig 80) Trachoni – Andry far left/her nephew Sami/Lina/Andry's mother Loukia (1980)

Fig 81) Wedding of cousin Stella in Paphos – Andry to the left of the bride and Telos to the right in the year of his death in 1980

Fig 82) Pinou – dressed in black at Stella's wedding in 1980

Fig 83) Andry holding Lina at Throni – Tomb of Makarios – 1980

Fig 84) Photo of Stella with her father Telos, and mother Kyriacou (in red) at her wedding – 1980

Fig 85) Trachoni – Lina's 3rd birthday party – Andry at rear (1981)

Fig 86) Green Monday – Andry far left (1981)

Fig 87) Trachoni - Andry and Anthoulla (1981)

Fig 88) Trachoni – Andry's father/Michalis on the bike of her former husband Christakis (1981)

Fig 89) Bus overturned in a dam near to Moniatis Village

(13.3.1981) Cyprus Mail

Fig 90) Bus overturned in a dam near to Moniatis Village

Fig 91) Green Monday (circa 1981) – Andry rear second from right

Fig 92) Trachoni - Andry's birthday (circa 1982)

Fig 93) Trachoni – Andry on her scooter (1982)

Fig 94) Andry finishing school (1983)

Fig 95) Andry finishing school (1983)

Fig 96) The class of 6th grade Lycium – Ayios Antonis, Limassol – Andry front row far right (1983)

Fig 97) Trachoni - The birthday of Andry's former husband Christakis (1983)

Fig 98) Andry's father Costas on her first wedding day (1983)

Fig 99) The wedding of Andry Christou to Christakis Christou 9 October 1983

Fig 100) Andry with her mother Loukia and a picture of her mother's wedding day (2017)

Fig 101) Andry with her four children – Andry/Valentinos/Lenos/Marios/Loukia (2011)

Fig 102) Andry with her brother and sisters Michalis/Despo/Andry/Chrystalla/Roulla/Maro (2007)

Fig 103) Andry with her father Costas (May 2016)

Fig 104) Andry with her granddaughter Christina (May 2016)

Fig 105) Andry with her mother Loukia (May 2016)

Fig 106) Andry with Christina and husband and co-author Michael Layton (May 2016)

Acknowledgments/References

Published by Stephen Burrows *(Bostin Books* and author)

'A Business of Some Heat' (2004) by Brigadier Francis Henn

'A History of Cyprus' (2002) by Dr Kypros Tofallis

'A Journey Through the Painted Churches of Cyprus' (2008) by Monk Dometios

Anthoulla Agathogleous – school-friend

'Bank of Cyprus Diary' (2004) with submissions from the Bank of Cyprus Cultural Foundation Cyprus Mail – and with special thanks to reporter George Psyllides

'Cyprus 1974 – the Greek coup and the Turkish Invasion' (2009) by Makarios Drousiotis cyprusisland.net

Panayiota Christodolou – school-friend

Alekos Constantinous – school-friend

Lefki Giasoumi – school-friend

Andry Ioannou – school-friend

'Journal of the Police History Society' – number 29(2015)

'Limassol – The Ballad of my Town' published by Andreas Neocleos

Malcolm 'Doc' Halliday – former corporal in the First Battalion of The Royal Scots Mydestinationcyprus.com

Koulla Mylonas – friend

Lydia Pelopida – school-friend

Tasos Charalambous – brother-in-law

The Times – 25 January 2017 edition

'The Time Machine Magazine' – Cyprus Edition

Trachoni Community Council – website

'The Cyprus Liberation Struggle - 1955 – 1959' - by Elenitsa Seraphim-Loizou.

'Violence in the Sun' – a history of football violence in Cyprus (2015) by Michael Layton *'When The Tanks Started'* by Androu Kiriakidi and Renou Prenza (1976)

Wikipedia

David Woolmer – former Royal Air Force & British Transport Police member

Biographies

Androulla Christou-Layton was born in Paphos Hospital in Cyprus on the 5 November 1965 and is one of six children. She was married to her first husband Christakis in 1983 and has four children from the marriage. Christakis passed away suddenly in 2005. Andry has previously worked in an office, as a sales representative, a beautician, and in a packing house.

Between 2000 and 2005 she was a police constable in the Sovereign Bases Police in Cyprus. She was one of only a small number of female officers to be trained in public order tactics and was the first female member of the Forces Marine Section at its inception. In 2012 she married her second husband Michael and moved to England where she now runs her own beauty business. Andry reads and writes English fluently. This is her first venture into writing.

Michael Layton QPM joined the British Transport Police as a Cadet on the 1 September 1968 and, after three years, was appointed as a Police Constable in 1971, serving at Birmingham

New Street Station. In 1972 he transferred to Birmingham City Police, which amalgamated in 1974 to become the West Midlands Police, where he eventually reached the rank of Chief Superintendent in 1997.

On retirement from that Force in 2003 he went on to see service with the Sovereign Bases Police in Cyprus, and then returned to the British Transport Police in 2004, initially as a Detective Superintendent (Director of Intelligence), and then in his last two years as the Operations Superintendent at Birmingham, where he continued with his passion for combating football violence, until finally retiring again in 2011.

In the January 2003 New Year's Honours List he was awarded the Queens Police Medal for distinguished police service. He is the co- author of a book entitled '*Hunting the Hooligans – the true story of Operation Red Card*' which was published in July 2015 by Milo Books, and the author of '*Violence in the Sun – a History of Football Violence in Cyprus*' which was published as an EBook also by Milo in May 2015.

In 2016/17 he has also co-authored *'Tracking the Hooligans – A history of football violence on the UK rail network'*, *'Police Dog Heroes'*, and *'The Hooligans Are Still Among Us'*, and authored *'Birmingham's Front Line'* all published by Amberley Publishers. He has also co-written books titled *'Black Over Bill's Mother's'* as well as *'The Noble Cause'*, *'Keep Right On'* and *'Walsall's Front Line'* with Stephen Burrows. Michael is a self-employed consultant engaged predominantly with crime and community safety issues. He married Andry in 2012 and they live in the UK.

Dedications

Androulla Christou-Layton: To my husband Michael for his determination and dedication to publish this book. To my mother Loukia, who has been *'my rock'* and has supported me, without ever judging me, throughout my entire life. To my father Costas for the *'colour'* that he put into my life and his continuing support. To my sisters and brother, who all feature in the book, and to my children Valentinos, Marios, Lenos, and Loukia – and of course my beautiful grand daughter Christina.

Michael Layton: To Andry for her love and commitment, and to my families in the UK and Cyprus.

PLEA FROM THE AUTHOR

Hello dear reader. Thank you for reading to the end of the book, we hope that means that you enjoyed it. Whether or not you did, we would just like to thank you for buying it, and giving us your valuable time to try and entertain you.

If you would like to find out more about our other fiction and non-fiction books then please search on our names on Amazon UK or go to *'Bostin Books'* Facebook page. We also have personal Facebook and Linkedin profiles

If you enjoyed this book we would be extremely grateful if you would consider leaving a review on Amazon.co uk, (or the Amazon site for your country). To do this, find the book page online, scroll down, and use the *'review button'*.

The most important part of a book's success is how many positive reviews it has, so if you leave one then you are directly helping and encouraging us to continue on our journey as authors. Thank you in advance to anyone who does.

22245839R00261

Printed in Poland
by Amazon Fulfillment
Poland Sp. z o.o., Wrocław